MW00425435

Early
Days
in
Texas

Jim McIntire *(From the Western History Collections, University of Oklahoma Library)*

Early Days in
TEXAS

A Trip to Hell and Heaven

By Jim McIntire

Edited with an Introduction and Notes
by Robert K. DeArment

University of Oklahoma Press
Norman and London

By Robert K. DeArment

Bat Masterson: The Man and the Legend (Norman, 1979)
Knights of the Green Cloth: The Saga of the Frontier Gamblers (Norman, 1982)
George Scarborough: The Life and Death of a Lawman on the Closing Frontier (Norman, 1992)

Text design by Patsy Willcox

Library of Congress Cataloging-in-Publication Data

McIntire, Jim, 1846–ca. 1910.
    Early days in Texas : a trip to hell and heaven / by Jim McIntire ; edited
with an introduction and notes by Robert K. DeArment. — 1st ed.
       p.   cm.
    Reprint. Originally published: Kansas City, Mo. : McIntire Pub. Co.,
c1902.
    Includes bibliographical references and index.
    ISBN 0-8061-2407-5 (alk. paper)
    1. McIntire, Jim, 1846–ca. 1910.   2. Pioneers—Texas—Biography.
3. Frontier and pioneer life—Texas.   4. Texas—Biography.
I. DeArment,   Robert K., 1925– . II. Title.
F391.M93   1992
976.406′1′092—dc20
[B]   91-30547
                                           CIP

The paper in this book meets the guidelines for permanence and durability of the Committee on Production Guidelines for Book Longevity of the Council on Library Resources, Inc.♾

Contents

	Acknowledgments	vii
	Editor's Introduction	3
	Author's Preface	9
I.	My Start in Life	11
II.	How I Became a Cowboy	15
III.	Life on the Ranch	20
IV.	Indian Atrocities	28
V.	Winter on the Ranch	31
VI.	Hunting Buffalo for Profit	36
VII.	With the Rangers	49
VIII.	Weeding Out the Outlaws	61
IX.	Running a Saloon in Texas	65
X.	Life in New Mexico	72
XI.	Captured by the Rangers	86
XII.	Again in the Toils	92
XIII.	In a Shooting Scrape	97
XIV.	Through Hell and Heaven	103
XV.	Conclusion	113
	Notes	117
	Bibliography	161
	Index	169

Acknowledgments

I would like to express my gratitude for assistance in the preparation of this book first of all to J. Evetts Haley and his very capable librarian, Beth Schneider, for the use of the copy of Jim McIntire's *Early Days in Texas: A Trip to Hell and Heaven* in the Nita Stewart Haley Memorial Library, Midland, Texas.

Others who generously contributed information which aided greatly in the development of the notations include: Susan Anderson, Silver City, New Mexico; Donaly E. Brice, Texas State Library, Austin, Texas; Evlyn Broumley, Weatherford Public Library, Weatherford, Texas; Laurel E. Drew, Albuquerque Public Library, Albuquerque, New Mexico; Bob Ernst, Stillwater, Oklahoma; Mary Fellows, Kiowa County Historical Society, Hobart, Oklahoma; Gary Fitterer, Kirkland, Washington; Sara Hallier, Kansas City Public Library, Kansas City, Missouri; Janet Ingles, Deputy Clerk, Boyd County, Kentucky; Louise James, Woodward, Oklahoma; Dave Johnson, Indianapolis, Indiana; Dorothy Johnson, Panhandle-Plains Historical Museum, Canyon, Texas; Bob Knecht, Kansas State Historical Society, Topeka, Kansas; Fred L. Lee, Kansas City, Missouri; Jacqueline Dorgan Maketa, Albuquerque, New Mexico; Rebecca Morrison, Public Library of Wichita Falls, Texas; Chuck Parsons, South Wayne, Wisconsin; J. Richard Salazar, State Records Center and Archives, Santa Fe, New Mexico; Diane Shelton, Kentucky Historical Society, Frankfort, Kentucky; Joe Todd, Oklahoma Historical Society, Oklahoma City, Oklahoma; Victor Westfall, Angel Fire, New Mexico; and the staff at the Toledo-Lucas County Public Library, Toledo, Ohio.

ROBERT K. DEARMENT

Sylvania, Ohio

Early
Days
in
Texas

A Trip to Hell and Heaven

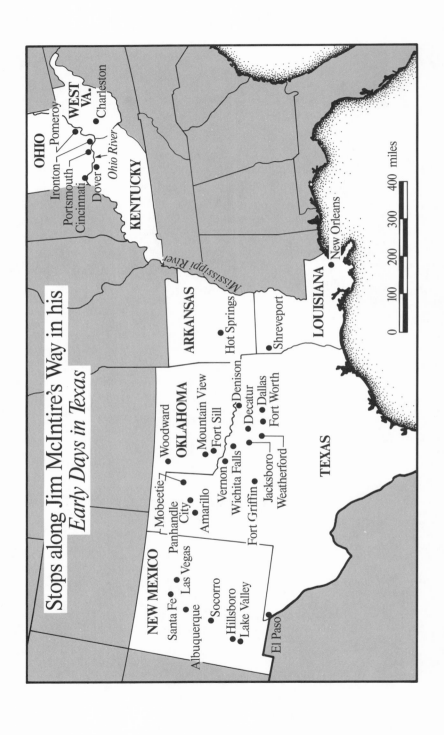

Stops along Jim McIntire's Way in his *Early Days in Texas*

Editor's Introduction

Ironically, the very event that prompted Jim McIntire to write and publish the story of his life, *Early Days in Texas: A Trip to Hell and Heaven,* has kept his book from being widely read. In 1901 McIntire contracted "black" or "Mexican" smallpox, the most malignant form of the disease, and he suffered what is now known as a "near-death experience" during which he felt that he had indeed died and that his spirit had departed his body. After recovery he was so impressed by his recollection of the supernatural journey that he set out to write it down. This account, replete with conversations with both Satan and God, was a remarkably juvenile description of his trip through the afterlife realms, in which he was pleased to learn that there were no children in Hell and that God found no harm in either gambling or the selling of whiskey. With an opportunity to question the Almighty regarding the philosophical perplexities that have plagued humanity throughout history, he chose to enumerate for God the days of the week and inquire with regard to their importance. In effect, God shrugged.

Not surprisingly, this childish narration found little readership. Since 1902, when McIntire privately published his book, no other editor or publisher has chosen to offer it again to the public.[1] Fortunately, however, McIntire confined the recitation of his feverish fantasies to the last chapter, a segment comprising only 20 pages of a 229-page volume.

McIntire devoted more than 90 percent of the book to recounting his life from his birth in the hill country of southern Ohio and his Huck Finn–like experiences on the Ohio River to his adventures in Texas and New Mexico during the last three decades of the nineteenth century. Throughout a life packed with action and excitement, McIntire was in turn cowboy, Indian fighter, buffalo hunter, Texas Ranger, sheepherder, saloonkeeper, deputy sheriff, boomtown policeman, town marshal, deputy United States marshal, hunted fugitive with a price on his head, jailhouse escapee, and professional gambler.

Although he encountered many famous and fascinating individuals and witnessed important events, his descriptions are at times irritating in their paucity. Nevertheless, he often provided details that add to our knowledge of this uniquely dramatic and colorful period of American history. A host of notable and colorful frontier figures parade through his narrative: early Texas rancher James C. Loving; successful pioneer businessmen Ira Rinehart, N. F. Locke, and George B. Berry; military men Henry O. Flipper and Albert J. Fountain; political dignitaries Lionel A. Sheldon and John A. Logan; legendary lawmen Pat Garrett, John W. Poe, and Wyatt Earp; and an assortment of outlaws, gunfighters, and badge-toters turned bad men that includes Sam Bass, John Larn, Dave Rudabaugh, "Billy the Kid" Bonney, "Mysterious Dave" Mather, Jim Courtright, and Milton J. Yarberry.

McIntire wrote of violent times and brutal events. His accounts, rendered in a simple, matter-of-fact style, are sometimes extremely gory; he probably delighted in upsetting the squeamish. He seldom included dates, and when he did, he was invariably incorrect, often unaccountably so.[2] He was much better with proper names, and the errors that recur, (for example, "Paliponte" for Palo Pinto and "State Plains" for Staked Plains) suggest that McIntire may have dictated his manuscript to a scribe unfamiliar with the regional geography. I have tried in the notes to rectify McIntire's errors and omissions and to amplify those areas in which his account is less than complete.

Since so few have ever read his book, today's students of the Old West usually remember McIntire for his association with Jim Courtright, a better-known Texas figure, and for his implication with Courtright in the infamous American Valley murders. Depictions of McIntire by later writers have been based, almost without exception, on the acerbic characterization set down by Charles A. Siringo, Texas cowboy, longtime Pinkerton agent, and inveterate autobiographer. Siringo, like McIntire, nearly died from a bout with smallpox, but had the wit not to include feverish hallucinations in any of the five book-length accounts he penned of his own life.

Claiming to have known McIntire well, Siringo labeled him "a plain killer" and equated him with the noted desperado Sam Bass. Writing in 1927, Siringo said McIntire was "another badman cowboy of the old school [who] had shot and killed several men before he came to the Texas Panhandle in the middle seventies."[3] Eugene Cunningham, a popular writer of Western fiction, echoed this depiction a few years later, referring to McIntire as "a very well known Panhandle gunman, a killer of very nervous trigger fingers."[4] J. Marvin Hunter, a pioneer historian of gunslinger lore, repeated this representation in 1951, describing McIntire as "a noted Texas Panhandle gunman and killer."[5] Later writers accepted these characterizations, although neither Siringo, Cunningham, Hunter, nor anyone since has provided details of specific incidents which might have been the basis for McIntire's supposed fearsome reputation, other than his involvement in the American Valley affair. This incident, which took place long after his reputation reportedly had been established, provides the one instance of his implication in a killing.

In *Early Days in Texas*, McIntire chose not to relate his side of that infamous affair; rather, he obfuscated the story by mixing it up with other issues. He described only a single gunfight in which he personally participated, one that took place late in his career, and one in which no one was killed. After surviving years on the raw edge of the Texas frontier, herding cattle, hunting buffalo, fighting Indians, and serving several stints with the Texas Rangers, McIntire undoubtedly acquired a reputation as a tough, resourceful fellow who knew his way around guns and gunmen. Jobs in law enforcement drew men of this stripe. Unencumbered by any romantic notion that as a lawman he could contribute to the taming of the West, McIntire pinned on a badge as a means of making a living. For one in that line of work the reputation of being a swift-handed gunslinger, a killer of men, was useful; it helped in securing appointment to the job and later

in controlling hard-case types. During the 1870s and 1880s when
McIntire served at various times as a lawman at all levels of government—municipal, county, state and federal—he may well
have welcomed a "killer" reputation. By 1902, after retiring
from those zones of conflict, he found this notoriety no longer
useful and ignored it in his book.

In addition to a quick-gun reputation, McIntire brought to
his frontier law enforcement career an imposing physical presence. In 1885 a newspaper described him as "a remarkably fine
looking young man about thirty years of age. He is six feet tall,
erect and broad-shouldered, and has a pair of dark, keen, fighting
eyes. The expression on his face is anything but forbidding, and
his manners are very quiet, his address pleasant, and taken all in
all, he doesn't look like a bully or desperado, although he does
look as if he would be a bad customer if he were aroused." [6]

Charlie Siringo wrote that he "was of a nervous disposition.
When angry, his slender frame shook like a leaf and his black
eyes sparkled with rage." [7] The single extant photograph of McIntire reveals a young man of good features, dark, well-groomed
hair, luxuriant black mustache and goatee, and those "dark, keen,
fighting eyes" the newsman and Siringo found most notable.

McIntire's unabashed racism pervaded the book. He took
every opportunity to deprecate the blacks with whom he came in
contact, from the members of his "nigger" minstrel troupe on
the Ohio and "their thirst for apple-jack and home-made whisky
[which] consumed the lion's share of the box-office receipts," to
a contingent of black cavalrymen from Fort Richardson who, he
said, could not be kept quiet on the trail of marauding Indians
"as they would rather have frightened the Indians away by their
noise than have defeated them in battle." He found it "laughable" in the midst of an Indian battle at the Loving ranch, when
a big cowboy, "in a spirit of fun," grabbed "a little colored
boy. . . . and held him up between himself and the Indians. How
that boy did squeal!" McIntire discovered "it was a hard matter

to fight with a little 'nigger' squealing fit to kill and no time to stop and laugh."

Hispanics commanded no greater respect, and McIntire referred to them by the contemptuous term "greasers." He was obviously unaware of the ludicrous nescience of his statement that in Las Vegas, New Mexico, he "was the only native officer, all the rest being 'Greasers.' " He contemptuously noted that Albert Fountain, who headed a militia company composed of "an ordinary, murderous lot of 'Greasers,' " was "an American who had married a Mexican."

His scorn spared no ethnic group: he referred to Chinese as "Chinks" and noted that they were often robbed, as "a Chinaman [was] always . . . considered legitimate prey in this country." He proudly boasted of brutalizing a Chinese cook who had angered him, grabbing the man by the queue and threatening to behead him with his penknife: "After another drink of whisky, I decided not to kill him, [but] cut his queue off and then kicked him off the porch. The 'Chink' was almost scared to death."

McIntire shared the almost universal view of Texas frontiersmen that Indians were subhuman, dangerous, treacherous creatures distinguished by their uncleanliness and "a sort of wet-dog odor which the horses don't like." Not surprisingly this contempt for living Indians extended to utter disrespect for the burial sites of dead ones: "The boys on the frontier never failed to rifle an Indian's grave every time they found one." When dismantling one of these cairns, he noted, he would find it inhabited by "the usual big gray rat that is always found in an Indian's grave," but does not suggest how the rat could distinguish an Indian's grave from a white's. While looting one such burial site, McIntire found the dead Indian's "teeth and finger-bones were so white and perfect" that he kept them "for ornaments." He told of skinning a "squaw" killed after a battle, tanning the hide, and making a purse which he carried for nine years.

Confessing to being "the hardest-hearted sinner on earth,"

who had "done everything that was good, also everything that was bad," McIntire still felt that he had been "charitable to everybody, and never saw anyone suffer if [he] could help it."

Unanswered questions still surround the life of McIntire. Although he mentions a wife several times within the book, he gives no information regarding whom he married, where and when the wedding took place, or if any children resulted from the union. Very little is known of his life after publication of *Early Days in Texas.*

Siringo, in a letter written in 1923, dismissed the book as "bum," and alleged that "Jim was an opium fiend when he wrote it."[8] He repeated the narcotic addiction charge in his 1927 book *Riata and Spurs,* saying that McIntire "finally became a dope fiend in El Paso, Texas, where he died a human wreck, in later years."[9] But Ramon Adams, that indefatigable challenger of every word written in the outlaw and lawman field, contended that Siringo stood unsupported in his depiction of McIntire as a dope fiend and that he was mistaken as to the place of death. "[McIntire] was living in Kansas City when he died," wrote Adams, uncharacteristically providing no source for his own assertion.[10]

Father Stanley Crocchiola, a Catholic priest who, under the pseudonym "F. Stanley," published many works based on extensive Western research, wrote that McIntire died in Canadian, Texas, in 1910 or 1911.[11] Later investigation, however, has led Crocchiola to believe that he died in a small town near Woodward, Oklahoma, between 1912 and 1916.[12] To this time no evidence has been found to confirm any of these reports or to establish a date and place for McIntire's demise.

Early Days in Texas: A Trip to Hell and Heaven, biased and flawed, somehow is an appropriate product of a man, also biased and flawed, who nevertheless recognized that he had led "a very busy life from boyhood" and whose experiences "very few men [had] gone through." Ignored for almost a century, it deserves to take its place among the important autobiographies of controversial frontier figures.

Author's Preface

Truth is often stranger than fiction, and my reason for publishing this volume is that my life is made up of a series of adventures beyond the comprehension of the average fiction writers. In these pages I have confined myself to facts as they occurred, and, after reading them, you will all agree that I have seen the life of two worlds as few have had the privilege of seeing. A number of those whose names appear in connection with my many adventures on earth are still living and enjoying prosperity in their respective communities. J. C. Loving, on whose ranch I received my first cowboy experience, is now president of the Live Stock Exchange of Ft. Worth, Texas; Cash Denny, my companion when I ran away from home to become a cowboy, is the proprietor of two prosperous meat markets in Denison, Texas; George Berry, who conducted the Junction Hotel at Washburn, Texas, is now an alderman of the Upper House in Kansas City, Mo.; John Poe, who was a deputy sheriff with me at Mobeetie, Texas, is now a banker at Roswell, N. M.; Mr. Reed, an intimate friend at Mobeetie, Texas, is now a general merchant at Whiteoaks, N. M.[1]

These men will know that I am relating facts in dealing with the frontier life of the Southwest, when they read this book.

My adventures began when I was a boy in Ohio, and then the scene is transferred to Texas and the Southwest. I have killed Indians and skinned them, chased outlaws across the plains with the Texas Rangers, hunted buffalo, enjoyed the hazardous life of a cow-puncher in the early days of Texas, run gambling houses and saloons, served as marshal and deputy sheriff in frontier towns, shot up towns and been mixed up in shooting scrapes, etc. I was also chased across three States with a reward of $1,000 on my head, dead or alive; was captured and broke jail, and have seen as much lawless life and had perhaps as many hair-raising adventures as any man living.

Besides an extraordinary life in this world, I was permitted to cross the river of death, view Heaven and Hell, and return to life again. In my fifty-first year[2] I was stricken with the black small-pox, from which I died. I have attempted to accurately describe all that I saw on that trip through the world which is to be our abiding-place after death, together with illustrations of the topography of both Heaven and Hell. I believe that it was the will of Providence which singled me out to visit the heavenly home of God and Satan's abode of misery and torture, then return to earth to enlighten the people in regard to the hereafter life.

By publishing these facts I believe that I am fulfilling a mission ordered by God and that every reader will be benefitted by a complete knowledge of all I was permitted to see.

In dedicating this book to the good sense of the American people, my only request is that it be received as a book of facts, not fiction nor an idle dream.

Respectfully,   JAMES MCINTYRE[3]

Woodward, O.T.

CHAPTER I

My Start in Life

I was born in the hills of Brown County, Ohio, in 1846.[1] My father and mother were plain country people and led a frugal life, which was the rule rather than the exception in that part of the country when I was a boy. Times were very hard and I was brought up on the plainest of fare and not overfed even on that. We never had coffee, but instead would parch corn and make a substitute for coffee, which, though not very palatable, had to do. I had the usual drudgery of farm life in a poor farming district until I was fourteen years old, when my father gave up farming and moved to Ironton.[2] My first situation was as a telegraph operator in the Western Union offices in Ironton, which was a thriving town at that time. I stayed with the Western Union Company about a year, when my father, seeing I was not looking strong, took me away and got me a job in a rolling-mill.

I was getting along very nicely in the rolling-mill and was being advanced as fast as any boy could expect, when one fine day a "nigger" minstrel troupe landed in town. At this time minstrel shows were the only class of theatricals that traveled through the smaller cities of the country, and, together with my chum, Johnny White,[3] we attended. They gave a very good entertainment, but their thirst for apple-jack and home-made whisky consumed the lion's share of the box-office receipts. Johnny and I were ambitious boys, and when the leader of the troupe told us his troubles, we began to figure on how we could embark into the show business. We asked him to make us a proposition on financing the show for a tour through southern Ohio, northern Kentucky and northwestern Virginia.[4] As he was in trouble and his "niggers" hadn't the where-with to procure anything more to drink, he made us what he called a very liberal offer, we had to pay the expenses and take half of the receipts. We promptly accepted and with boyish ambition completed our arrangements for a trip on the road. Johnny didn't have nuch [sic] money, but what he lacked in finance he made up by being a good fellow, and I furnished the major portion of the expense fund. Two days later

Johnny and I, without the consent of our parents or any one else, marched down to the boat-landing at the head of our newly acquired minstrel troupe. We walked up the gang-plank with the confidence of old theatrical managers, and were soon steaming up the Ohio, bound for Catlettsburg, Kentucky,[5] where we were to give our first performance. On arriving at Catlettsburg, we turned the "niggers" loose to wander around the streets until show time, while we hunted up the local printer and arranged to have five hundred hand-bills printed and distributed over the town, announcing the arrival of the great, world-famed minstrel troupe. There was no hall in the town, and we were at a loss to find a place where we could give a show. We finally approached the sheriff for the use of the court-house, and he readily gave his consent.[6] We told him a hard-luck story and got him to allow us to go ahead without putting up for the rent or the license fee, which we agreed to pay after the show. That sheriff was easy, and we showed to a full house two nights in succession. After the second night's performance, the "niggers" started out to load up on apple-jack and white lightning whisky. In a couple of hours they were hilarious and someone started a fight. They were mixing it up lively, when the sheriff and a couple of deputies swooped down on them and landed the whole bunch in jail. Just at this time Johnny and I appeared on the scene and gave the sheriff a good talk. He was one of those sheriffs who took talk instead of money, and it went. We stood good for the "niggers'" fines and told the sheriff that with another good night we could pay him in full. Things looked pretty blue for us and we were afraid we might have to pay the sheriff, which was against our principles. The next morning we wandered down to the river bank, where we saw two large skiffs that were not in use. Those skiffs suggested a way of stealing a march on the sheriff, so we went back up town, where we put in a long day. As soon as it was dark, we rounded up our black Thespians, bought a supply of eatables, consisting of Bologna sausage, crackers, and canned goods, and returned to the river. It did not take us long to load the "niggers" and food into the two skiffs and pull for the Ohio shore. We got away so quietly that they never missed us, and the people may have turned out a good house for us that night for all we ever knew.

Once on the Ohio side, we camped in an old house that had been almost shot to pieces by the gunboats during the John Morgan raid.[7] We were having lively times and leading a strenuous life for boys of our age. The next morning we walked to the nearest town, which was hardly large enough to enjoy a dot on the map, but we showed there that night and did very well.

Our next jump was to Gallipolis,[8] where we showed two nights. We were now on the high road to success, and took a big jump to Charlestown, West Virginia, a distance of about sixty miles.[9] We did our traveling by boat and were enjoying our experience as heartily as two sixteen-year-old boys could.[10] On arriving at Charlestown, we interviewed the sheriff and secured the court-house for a week's stand. Things came good for us and the "niggers" kept sober, so at the end of the week we were $1200 ahead on our venture. From Charlestown we thought we would try Colton, a coal-mining town a few miles east.[11] We secured a farmer with a wagon to haul our baggage overland and we walked behind the wagon. The roads were so bad that we could not ride. This was too much like work for our liking, but we were feeling pretty good with our pockets full of the shinplasters[12] we had cleared in Charlestown. Colton was the scene of the first real trouble we had. As it was just after the Civil War, the people of West Virginia had none too much love for the negroes, but those miners at Colton didn't have any at all, and they lost no time in showing it. As soon as the performance started on the first night a shower of missiles of every description came through the windows, creating consternation with the audience and actors alike. The mob howled on the outside and pelted the building with clubs and stones, threatening to break the doors in and kill the "niggers." After a time the mob quieted down and we got the "niggers" out through a rear entrance and got around to the hotel, where we hustled the "niggers" into the stable and locked them up for the night. We secured accommodations for ourselves at the hotel. We were up before daylight and got our badly scared troupe out of town. After holding a consultation, we concluded that the best place for a gentleman of color was on the north side of the Ohio River. We showed a couple of times on the way, but kept straight north until we reached the Ohio. When we crossed the river and the negroes felt the freedom of the Ohio atmosphere, they immediately filled up on apple-jack and refused to show. The novelty of managing a show was rapidly wearing away, and we had enough of colored minstrel aggregations, so we quietly took our departure, leaving the "niggers" in a jubilant state of intoxication. We started across the country afoot, well supplied with money, the profits of our West Virginia successes. As soon as the "niggers" got sober enough to miss us, they complained to the sheriff of the county, and five officers were put on our trail. They caught us and compelled us to return with them. As they could not do anything with us, they turned us loose, and the next morning we hired two horses and resumed our journey. In the meantime the sheriff got scared, as we had intimated that we would have them arrested for kidnaping, and he set out to overtake us. When he caught up with us, he rode along for some time without making any overtures, but we felt that he wanted to square himself in some way. When we came to a cross-roads, one of which led to a ferry, he said he thought he would make a trip over into Kentucky, but we forced him to go on with us to Ironton. A little farther on he asked us what we wanted to compromise the matter, and we told him that $100 was the least we would take. He finally offered to give us $80, return our hired horses, and pay the livery bill. We gladly accepted his terms, and went on into Ironton to our homes.

CHAPTER II

How I Became a Cowboy

I remained at home a few weeks and had one of the best times of my life. Johnny White, my partner on the road, and I were the heroes among our boy acquaintances around town, and as we had our pockets full of money with nothing to do but spend it, we passed many happy days. My next venture was steamboating on the Ohio River. I obtained a position as assistant to the pilot on the "Ohio No. 4," running between Pomeroy and Cincinnati, a distance of eighty miles.[1] I followed this for two years, and as the pay was good and the work easy, I liked it very much. I quit, however, and fell in with a character known as Happy Joe Jeffers, a canal-boatman on the Ohio Canal.[2] Happy Joe was all that his name would indicate. He was a genial, good-natured fellow, who was never seen except in a good humor and ready to laugh away his own troubles. He took a liking to me and I went with him. He owned his own canal-boat and made regular trips between Chilicothe and Portsmouth.[3] I spent about two months with Happy Joe floating produce down the Miami Canal,[4] and made good money. I was lost from my parents for two years, but was enjoying life, and that didn't worry me at all.

About this time Capt. Metcalf challenged Capt. Chapin to fight a duel. They were both officers in the Union Army stationed along the Ohio River, and the challenge was the result of a quarrel which had been hanging fire for some time. The duel was scheduled to take place at Dover, Kentucky, on a certain day, and for a week the people all over that part of the country were talking of nothing else. On the day of the duel the river was lined with people on both sides. I went along with Happy Joe. We had a good position to view the affair, and were close enough to hear the count and command to "fire" given. Both were armed with long-barreled dueling pistols, and were thirty paces apart. The place selected was a long, sandy beach, and as pretty a scene as there is on the Ohio River. When the seconds had completed all arrangements, the duelists stepped back thirty paces. The stillness was oppressive as the count, "One, two, three, fire!" rang out clear on that summer afternoon, and both fired. Chapin fell dead at the water's edge with a bullet through his heart, while Metcalf was untouched. A squad of soldiers carried Chapin's body to his former quarters, while Metcalf, after handing over his pistol, walked back to camp.[5] The crowd, after discussing the scene just witnessed for a few minutes, slowly dispersed and returned to their homes. While Happy Joe and I were working our way through the crowd on the return, I unexpectedly met my father, who had also come to see the duel, and he insisted on my going home with him.

Southern Ohio was a great chicken-fighting country at that time, and the sport is not dead there yet. When I was at home, I had nothing to do, and I liked to see the chickens perform with the spurs on. Well, to make a long story short, I got to fighting chickens as regularly as some people "shoot the can."[6] I was always on the lookout for a rooster that could fight and picked up some pretty good ones. Every night mill-men, nail-makers, and corner-loafers, to the number of forty or fifty, would assemble in the basement of a grocery, and the fun would begin. Betting was never very heavy, as shinplasters were in circulation then, and amounts were small as compared with amounts wagered in the twentieth century. My father learned of my adventures with the birds and gave me a scolding that I shall never forget.[7]

About this time I had developed an ambition to be a cowboy and see life on the plains as portrayed by the dime novels I had been reading. I could not get over my father's scolding, and as another boy, whose name was Cash Denny, had ambitions along the same line, we ran away from home together.[8] Denny is at present the proprietor of two prosperous meat markets in Denison, Texas. We first went to New Orleans, but did not stop there long, as we were anxious to get into the cow country.

From New Orleans we went up the Red River to Shreveport, Louisiana, and from there walked along with some bull teams to the place where Dallas, Texas, now stands. Dallas was but a straggling village then. There were only a few houses, a mere

trading-point for the cattle-men. There wasn't a railroad nor a
fence in the whole State of Texas, and we were where our cow-
punching ambitions could be gratified. [9] We were not overbur-
dened with baggage, as Cash could easily take care of his one
extra shirt, while I had only an extra pair of pants to look after. I
had all the money, which consisted of a two-dollar bill. We were
not much worried over our finances, but when I found a roll of
shinplasters which contained three dollars and fifty cents, we
were full of enthusiasm. Our enthusiasm led us to purchase a link
of Bologna sausage and start for Ft. Worth. At the time we
reached Ft. Worth the town consisted of one house. [10] Old Man
Terrel lived there and kept a feed-yard, where we secured lodg-
ings for the night. [11] The next morning found us on our way to
Weatherford. As we were coming into the Indian country, we
began to feel just a little nervous at times. Whenever we came to
a creek, we would pull out our little four-barreled pistols and
investigate. We were very cautious, as we had read in our yellow
books how cautious Indian-fighters were. When night overtook
us, we found a house which was inhabited by an old gray-haired
man and woman. They were of the old rebel sort and wouldn't let
us stay all night, because we were from the North. It was hard to
have to pull out and "hit" the plains for the night, and as we were
awful hungry, as boys will sometimes become under similar conditions, I shot one of the old man's young pigs, which got in the
way of my pistol. We built a fire and were preparing to hold a
high carnival over the roast pig, when the old man set his bulldog
on us. As we did not care to have the dog make a supper off of
us, we ran away, leaving the pig on the fire. We did not care to
pass up the old man's generous hospitality entirely, so, after it
was good and dark, we crept back and registered for a night's
lodging in the haystack. We were hungry and tired all at once,
and could have thoroughly appreciated a nice warm meal at
home. While we were thinking over our misfortunes, a noise on
the outside of the stack startled us. We thought of the Indians,
and our hair assumed a Pompadour aspect. However, we got our

guns ready, and, on peering out, saw that it was a man. We spoke to him, and he answered in a white man's voice, which sort of acted as a safety-valve on our throbbing hearts. It turned out to be a humpbacked peddler, and we were so glad that it wasn't an Indian that we welcomed him to share our castle.

We were two hungry boys when we awoke next morning, but not any hungrier than the peddler who shared the haystack with us. We didn't stop to prepare much of a toilet, but set out early for Weatherford, the peddler accompanying us. His pack was heavy and his stomach light. He grumbled continuously, which did not do much toward making things cheerful. We trudged along, however, determined to make Weatherford by night. We had not traveled far until we found a big new dishpan which had fallen from a passing wagon. We carried this along, hoping that we would find an opportunity or two for using it. A few miles farther on the opportunity came, for as we were passing a grove we noticed a company of negroes preparing breakfast after having spent the night in the grove. We could think of nothing but how hungry we were, and the bacon the negroes were broiling smelled awfully good. We made them a proposition to trade our dishpan for some bacon and corn bread, and, as dishpans were valuable assets on the frontier of Texas, we had no trouble in reaching an agreement. With a fairly good supply of corn bread and bacon under our belts, we "hit" the road for Weatherford again. After tramping all day without anything further in the way of food disturbing our stomachs, we landed in Weatherford[12] about dark, a little more tired and a little more homesick than when we registered at the strawstack. We cut loose from the peddler and went to the old Blackwell Hotel, where we got supper and a good bed.[13] The Blackwell Hotel was a two-dollar house and we had only a two-dollar bill between us, but we put up a bold front and did not allow such little things as becoming stranded to worry us. However, we were so tired that we went to bed soon after supper. We got up early the next morning and started out to look for work. I ran into J. C. Loving, a stock man, who was hiring all the men he could get to protect the cattle on his ranch from the depredations of the Indians.[14] I struck him for a job for myself and companion, and, as we were likely-looking youngsters, he hired us. We went back to the hotel in high spirits over our good luck, especially as the work was right in line with the yellow-backed novels we had read back in Ohio. After settling up with the landlord, we joined Loving for a trip to the ranch.

The Indians were pretty bad at that time, and their boldness in committing depredations was alarming. There were all kinds of stories floating around the town about how the Indians were attacking the ranches and killing and burning as they went. These stories were not exaggerated either, for on one occasion they rode into Weatherford and drove off all the horses hitched to the court-house hitching-rack in the center of the town. This little incident of frontier life had happened just a few days before our arrival in Weatherford, and was a sample of what we could expect in the future.

Loving's ranch was in the Big Loss Valley[15] in Jack County, where the Indians were the worst. After he had hired all the men he could pick up, we started for the ranch. There were about thirty-five men in the party, and with a large number of horses and several supply-wagons we started out in true Texas frontier style. The journey to the ranch was made without incident, except while we were passing through Jacksboro[16] we saw two dead men lying on the sidewalk who had been killed in a dance-hall row the night before.[17] The scene was too much for our "tender-foot" hearts, and we would gladly have exchanged the adventures of ranch life for the comforts of home. But there was no turning back now, and we kept our places in the procession until we arrived at the ranch about the middle of the afternoon.

CHAPTER III

Life on the Ranch

Loving's ranch, which was to be the scene of many exciting adventures, was about twenty miles long and ten miles wide, occupying the entire Big Loss Valley. The valley was surrounded on all sides with wooded hills and lonesome peaks, and the afternoon our eyes first rested upon it, the cattle and buffalo were grazing contentedly in the distance, making as beautiful a scene as could be found in the whole State of Texas. The peaceful appearance was but an illusion, however, as the Indians were too plentiful to keep still long at a time. Away to the right lay the ranch buildings, corral, etc. The buildings were situated on Clear Creek, whose branches watered the valley. Clear Creek derived its name from the clear water which flowed between its banks, and was the home of the finest black bass I ever saw. The buildings were built by driving posts into the ground so close together that they made stockade houses, and consisted of Mr. Loving's residence, the ranch quarters, and a smoke-house. The houses were roofed with bark and were made as comfortable as possible for the facilities at hand.

We were now right in the heart of the Indian country, surrounded by hostile Kiowas and Commanches. We took to ranch work all right, and for a month everything went well. We were always on the lookout, however, and traveled in groups. We were constantly hearing of Indian depredations, and often found signs showing where they had passed in the night. Loving's ranch was the outpost of civilization, and was the first ranch the Indians had to pass in going from the Reservation to the settlements.

March 17, 1869,[1] was the day for a general round-up, and a number of cow-punchers came over from Jacksboro to help out.[2] They camped just across the creek, about two hundred yards from the ranch, and prepared to eat dinner before starting on the big cow-hunt. Our horses were grazing close to the camp, and I was in the house with the rest of our boys, eating dinner, when a shot was fired from behind the corral.[3] Thirty-five Indians had crept up and taken positions behind the corral. In an instant everything was excitement and everybody trying to get a line on the Indians. On the ranch firing a shot was the recognized signal that Indians were approaching, and the Jacksboro boys immediately leaped to their saddles. The Indians had anticipated this move on the part of the cow-punchers, and held their guns aimed at the saddles. John Heath was the first one to reach his horse, and had just placed one foot in the stirrup when he went down, hit by a Spencer bullet which entered the head just over the left eye. The horses then broke for the ranch corral. Here it was that I got my first taste of Indian fighting, and I plunged into the thickest of it. When the horses started for the corral, we were making it warm for the Indians, and succeeded in holding them at bay. One Indian, however, started for the horses in the attempt to prevent them from entering the corral. Loving saw his game and started after him, and succeeded in turning the horses into the corral. It was a thrilling sight to see Loving and the Indian race for the horses, exchanging shot for shot. After each shot they would wait a few seconds, watching each other intently, to determine if the other was hit. By this time we had beaten the other Indians back, and they were off in a bunch. We then turned our attention to the duel between Loving and the lone red man, but, as it was a fair fight, neither one having an advantage, we did not interfere. Finally the Indian wheeled his horse around and galloped up the creek to where we had a fine big saddle-horse hobbled. As he drew near the horse he threw his lasso, and at the same time whipping out his knife, cut the hobbles as he was passing. This was all done while riding at full gallop, and under the fire of thirty-five guns. Having captured the horse, he joined the rest of the Indians. The Indians, baffled in their first attempt, again drew closer and opened fire. Mrs. White, Loving's sister-in-law,[4] loaded guns for me, and I took a position under a big oak tree in the yard, firing at the approaching Indians as fast as she could load the guns. Inside the house there was a large gun-rack, which was kept filled with loaded guns for use in the Indian raids, and I had these in reserve, so I could keep shooting as fast as I could take aim and fire. Bullets were flying thick and fast around me, as the greater part of their fire was directed at me and Mr. Loving, who was between the Indians and the corral where all the horses were. All the rest were mounted and had to load their own guns, so it fell to me to do the most of the firing, as Mrs. White was an adept at loading. The Indians tried hard to hit us, knowing that if they had Loving and me out of the way, they could cut the rest off from the corral and sweep down and capture the horses. We were fighting at from two hundred to five hundred yards, and our Henry and Spencer rifles were not very effective at that range, as it was impossible to shoot with any degree of accuracy. The coolest one of the whole party was Mrs. White, who loaded guns and handed them out to me just as if that were her regular business. Her three little children were in the house, but not even a thought of the danger they were in affected their nerves. At last all but two Indians had withdrawn from the fight, and they were sitting on their horses near the corral where they shot Heath. Mrs. White thought they might be dislodged by a big old-fashioned foreign-made gun which shot a very large bullet. She handed this out to me saying, "Here is a big gun; try them two setting on their horses." I laid down, taking careful aim, and fired high. When I fired, one of the horses jumped, and the Indian, slapping his horses's side, wheeled and galloped away, patting his back at me. It was really amusing, and Mrs. White "gave me the merry ha! ha!" as they would call it in Kansas City. She laughed good and hard. I don't know whether it was at me or the Indian, but I never saw her laugh so heartily in time of peace.

When the last Indian had gone, we took an inventory of the fight, and found that it had lasted about half an hour and we had one man fatally wounded. The Indians succeeded in getting their wounded away with them, so we could never tell how much damage we inflicted. A laughable incident occurred in the first part of the fight, when a little colored boy the Jacksboro boys had brought over to cook for them started for the supply-wagon to get his gun. A big fellow named Henson[5], in a spirit of fun, grabbed up the little black urchin and held him up between himself and the Indians. How that boy did squeal! The boys all thought the Indians had hit him and insisted on Henson letting him go, as it was a hard matter to fight with a little "nigger" squealing fit to kill and no time to stop and laugh.

The boys lost no time in caring for John Heath, who was still alive. They carried him to the ranch, a distance of two hundred and fifty yards, where they tenderly laid him down. The brains were oozing out of the wound in the forehead, and it could be seen at a glance that he was not long for this world. He was unconscious and life quickly ebbed away.[6] The boys dug a grave, wrapped the body in blankets, and consigned it to Mother Earth. On top of the body was placed a lot of sticks, as boards were unheard of on Texas ranches in the sixties, and the earth was thrown in on top of the sticks.

The boys were then divided into two squads, one of which started in pursuit of the Indians and the other was left to guard the ranch. It fell to my lot to remain at the ranch. I climbed the big oak tree under which I had a half-hour before poured a hot fire into the ranks of the Indians, and acted as a look-out. From this position I had a full view of the entire valley. The Indians did not come back, however, and we spent the time quietly watching until the other party returned. Late in the evening the boys came in, leading a white horse covered with blood.[7] They had followed the Indians up into the mountains to the northwest of the ranch, where they came upon the horse, which belonged to the Indians. Where the horse was captured there was blood all over the rocks, but no Indian could be found. The horse was a fine animal, and he was named "Whiteman."

After the excitement of the Indian raid died away, everything at the ranch ran smoothly for some time. One evening a Mexican by the name of Lorenzo and a fellow-rancher named White[8] went to the upper end of the valley to drive the cattle out of the timber, so they would not become mixed with the wild cattle which ran there. The two separated to hunt up the cattle, and in due time the Mexican returned, but White failed to show up. White was riding a racing pony and should have been back at least as soon as the Mexican, so the boys suspected foul play. The next morning we took the Mexican to the place where they separated. From there we followed White's trail for a distance of two miles. We found where White had ridden up to within fifty feet of a bunch of seven Indians, who were hidden behind a small hill. The trail showed where he had wheeled his horse and broke for the Big Rocky Mountains. The length of the strides also showed that he was just "hitting the high places." He must have been outrunning the Indians, as he left the mountains and turned toward the ranch. Then the Indians split and ran in the shape of a letter V. White had a good horse, and this fact must have made him careless, as his horse fell in a ditch, allowing the Indians to overtake him. They killed and scalped him, cut all the leather off his saddle, and took the saddle-tree and his horse. I picked up a large and very fine ostrich plume, which had been lost by one of the Indians. White had lain in the sun all day, and decomposition had already set in. We brought the body in to the ranch and buried him beside Heath. These were two funerals at which few tears were shed, but all the boys' hearts were full of sorrow just the same, and the tenderness and respect shown for the dead was just as marked as I have ever seen anywhere.[9]

A few days after the tragic ending of White we had occasion to get the cattle out of the timber again. Four of us were in the party, and it was a drizzling, rainy day. We saw an object in the timber some distance away which looked like a bunch of cattle, and we started for them. When we were about a mile from them, one of the boys yelled: "Boys, that is not cattle!" But we kept on, and soon discovered that what we took for a bunch of cattle was in reality a band of Indians, mounted, but leaning over their horses' necks in order to make their forms as difficult to distinguish as possible. They were about one hundred yards out from the timber and watching our movements carefully. There was a creek about a quarter of a mile from the point where the Indians were, which was bounded on each side by high bluffs, with a nice little valley stretching away towards the ranch. We kept right on until we got under the bluff, out of sight of the Indians, when we cut loose for the ranch as fast as our horses could travel. When we had ridden about a half-mile, we pulled up and looked back. As the Indians were not aware of the fact that we had discovered their presence and played a little trick upon them, they made a charge on the bluff at the point where they expected us to come out. As near as we could count, there were thirty of them, and we watered our horses while watching them make the charge. As soon as they discovered they had been tricked, they started after us, but we were a mile away before they got a good start. They waved at us to come back, and we stopped our horses to allow them a breathing-spell. They then fired a few shots at us and started again, but we thought discretion the better part of valor, and galloped home.

This band of Indians made away with twenty-three head of Loving's horses one night, but were not satisfied with that, as they stayed in the vicinity until they got over one hundred good horses.

Indians always go on a raid when the moon is full, and we could expect them just as regularly as the moon got full. We would take extra precautions, but they came in such numbers and so stealthily that they generally got away with something. So the next full moon came around, and another band of Indians with it. We had all the horses, guarding them along the pasture fence when the Indians came. The night was very dark and cloudy, and it required all the vigilance the men were capable of to protect the horses grazing under their charge. Six men were detailed for this duty, and they divided the time into three watches, with two men on watch at a time. When Pat Sweeney and his partner were on watch, two Indians sneaked into the pasture and "swiped" a few horses. They located the boys and the main bunch of horses, and planned to get between the horses and the fence and stampede them. Sweeney's eagle eye spied them, and, although it was too dark to distinguish their figures, he was sure they were Indians. Riding up, he commanded them to halt, threatening to fire if they made another move. They kept on toward him and he opened fire on them. At the first shot the Indians wheeled their horses and started toward the ranch, with Sweeney and his men right after them. We heard the noise and ran out to head them off, but it was so dark we could not tell our boys from the Indians, and didn't dare shoot, although Sweeney kept yelling for us to do so. The Indians saw the ranch and turned off up the creek. They were on fresh horses they had stolen from the pasture, and galloped up the creek at breakneck speed. A couple of hundred yards from the ranch the Indians rode over a bluff, falling about thirty feet, and we gave up the chase for the night. There was a quantity of broken rock at the bottom of the precipice, and we expected to find Indians, horses and all, either killed or badly hurt. The next morning we examined the place where they went over, but the only thing to show where they lit was a little horse-hair on one of the stones. It was a miracle how they escaped.

The next night we drove the horses into the corral, knowing the Indians were still in the vicinity. That night we could hear them roaming over the prairie hooting like owls. Knute White, Loving's brother-in-law,[10] had a favorite horse, which he was afraid the Indians would get, and in order to keep it out of their reach, he tied it to the corner of the house. There was a big rail-fence around the house, and one Indian, a little more bold than the rest, crept up top the fence, and hid himself on the inside. White was laying for any attempt of the Indians to get his horse, and armed with a double-barreled shot gun, loaded with buck-shot, and a six-shooter, he stood guard. Along in the night the Indian came out from his hiding-place beside the fence and crawled up, untied the horse, and, leaping on his back, galloped off. White was so taken by surprise that he forgot all about his double-barreled shotgun, and began shooting after the fleeing Indian with his six-shooter. It is needless to remark that the Indian got away with the pet horse, and White was very much chagrined.[11]

CHAPTER IV

Indian Atrocities

In those days the buffalo would occasionally come down into the valley in immense herds, and when they left, large numbers of cattle mixed up with them would be forced to go along. Curtis Brothers, of Jacksboro,[1] had many cattle on the range with Mr. Loving's herds, and when the cattle would wander away in this way, they would furnish a number of men to go with Mr. Loving's men to separate them from the buffalo herds. Getting cattle out of a herd of buffaloes is exciting sport, and we enjoyed it better than anything in the way of ranch work. It was a grand sight to see the prairies black with buffalo almost as far as one could see. There were also wild horses and all kinds of game on the prairies, which added zest to the work. Our party had been out about two weeks and succeeded in reclaiming about two thousand cattle from the buffaloes. We shot game and had a good time in general. In fact, we did so much shooting that when we sighted a band of Indians we had only a few cartridges left in our belts. There was nothing to do but cut and run, so we started the cattle down the Clear Fork of the Brazos River and turned them loose. The Clear Fork was at swimming stage, so we swam our horses across. We then made for Fort Griffin, where all the good things of frontier life were to be had, such as whisky, tobacco, etc.[2] We took along plenty of whisky, inside and out, tobacco and cartridges. We then returned to the place where we turned the cattle loose, and succeeded in rounding up most of them. After the roundup, we killed some buffalo calves and had a barbeque of our own. The meat was delicious, and we enjoyed it more than some people do a dinner at Delmonico's. We then picked our teeth, and started for Graham City, which was one of the few Texas towns on the map.[3] When we arrived at Graham, we were in a swapping mood, and swapped a steer for some brandied cherries. Those cherries were very palatable, so palatable that we got gloriously drunk, and we lost our cattle again. With aching heads and parched throats, we started out to round them up once more. We found only a part of them, and then concluded we had better get them home before we lost them all.

One day Mr. Loving concluded to take a ride around the ranch. He took Carr Hunt, Shad Damon and Ed Newcomb along for company.[4] As they were riding along the opposite side of the valley, about nine miles from the ranch, they were surprised by a band of about one hundred and fifty Indians, who were looking for scalps and horses. They turned and ran into the timber. Proceeding along under cover until they reached a large and rocky promontory known as Lost Valley Peak, they ascended, completely throwing the Indians off their trail. They had outrun the Indians, as they had the best horses. Loving's policy was to keep the best horses that could be secured. Loving himself was mounted on a big Spanish horse about seventeen hands high—in fact, the biggest Spanish horse that I ever saw. As he was a very heavy man, he required a good, strong horse. Even this big Spanish horse gave out with him, and when he saw that the Indians had given up the chase, he had two of the boys double up, and they made a run for the ranch. leaving the Spanish horse and saddle on Lost Valley Peak. They could see the Indians away off in the valley, and they feared a raid on the ranch. Loving and his party were seven miles from the ranch when they made a dash for it. They made it all right, and I was stationed at the top of the big oak tree, to watch the band. They passed us up, however, and went on south through Jack, Montauk,[5] and Clay Counties, killing and stealing as they went. They wound up their trail of blood by crossing Red River and returning to the Reservation a few days later.[6] Among their depredations on this trip was the murder and mutilation of an old gray-haired man and woman. After killing them, they scalped them and mutilated their bodies terribly. They did not even spare the little four-year-old granddaughter, but ran a stake through her body and stuck it up on the fence which surrounded the house. At another point in the valley they killed a man by the name of Mason and his little boy. They then took Mrs. Mason up to the top of a small wooded hill, where they tied her to a tree, and nine of them ravished her. Not being satisfied with that, and seeing she was in a delicate condition, they cut her open and took her unborn babe, which they hacked to pieces with their knives. After this horrible butchery, they departed, leaving the half-dead woman tied to the tree. She was dead when found a day or two later.[7]

CHAPTER V

Winter on the Ranch

There were hundreds of wild cattle roaming over the Brazos River valley, and the first winter I spent on the ranch I had many opportunities to take a hand in their capture. It was a great sport, and I enjoyed it immensely. If we could not corral the wild cattle, we tried to drive them off the ranch, as they would lead our gentle cattle away, causing us much trouble to recover them. We built a corral with long wings extending out on two sides, just on the edge of the prairie glades where the cattle would come out at night to graze. In order to trap the wild cattle, we would pen up a number of the domesticated animals, leaving them in the corral all day without food. By night they would be very hungry, when we would let them out between the two wings of the corral to graze. Concealing ourselves in the cedar-brakes, we would then await the coming of the wild cattle, which kept under cover during the day. The wild cattle, seeing the tame ones grazing quietly, would come out among them. We would generally wait four or five hours, in order to give all that were coming an opportunity to get thoroughly mixed up with our own cattle; then we would surround the whole herd and stampede them into the corral. In this way we secured many good cattle and many that were as wild as deer and never could be tamed. Among them would be steers and cows eight and ten years old and so used to wild life that they had become too "foxy" to domesticate. In stampeding the cattle to the corral, occasionally several of the wilder ones would attempt to break through our line and get back to the cedar-brake. We would shoot these on the spot, and the balance, seeing the fate of their leaders, would not make any further attempt to get away. We sometimes got a few deer and antelope in the corral with the cattle, and it might be added that we had a taste for antelope, just like a "cullud pusson" has for 'possum.

Another regular job we had was keeping the wolves away from the cattle, as the big Lobo wolves did much damage to unprotected herds. They would travel in packs of fifty or seventy-five, and stealthily creep up to where the cattle were grazing, when they would divide into several packs, each pack singling out a nice fat steer or heifer. Most of them would rush at the unfortunate animal's head, while one would come up from the rear and hamstring it, rendering it entirely helpless and an easy victim to their prey. Whenever we would sight a pack of Lobo wolves, we lost no time in heading them away from the cattle. They never attacked a man, but it took many cattle to satisfy their appetites. There were also plenty of coyotes howling around, but no one ever paid any attention to them.

When Christmas came around, we needed more supplies, especially whisky. What would Christmas be on the ranch without whisky anyway? We did not propose to get along without it, and I was selected to go to Paliponte [1] for the goods. It wasn't half as hard a task to go to town for whisky and other supplies as it was to go for other supplies and no whisky. I hitched the team to a wagon we used to keep our horses' corn in, and set off alone. The wagon had a heavy oak top to keep the horses from getting the corn, and had I known the trouble it was destined to cause me, I would have been better prepared. The day was very cold, and a north wind was howling dismally across the valley. It began snowing a little as I neared the Brazos River, which had to be forded. The river was swift and high, and it was a case of swim for the horses, and get wet for me. I stopped, and got out to see what I could do in the way of keeping my wagon-bed and wagon together. Finding a short hitchrope, the only one I had with me, I tied it across the bed and around the sand-bolsters, and trusted to luck as to its being enough to hold things together. I wore a big overcoat, with cartridge-belt tied around me, and gloves.

It wasn't a pleasant task to survey, but I started in determined to get across at any cost, for I was going for frontier whisky for Christmas. I got along nicely until I struck deep water. Almost as soon as the horses began swimming I felt the lines tightening. I could not understand it, but eased up on the lines until I came to the end, when I knew there was something wrong. As the horses were swimming and the wagon floating, I could not see what the trouble was, so I turned the horses back to the side of the river where I started. When I struck shallow water, I discovered that the top of the wagon floated while the wheels kept to the bottom. The water had raised the bed and sand-bolsters high enough to become uncoupled and the bed and rear wheels stayed with me while the front wheels went with the horses. It was a nice condition to be in when the current was swift and no help nearer than the ranch. I got out into the water and made an attempt to get the bed back into place, but it was top-heavy and the swift water turned it over on me. I was handicapped with a heavy overcoat, which the current acted upon like a strong wind does on a sail; but the boys had to have refreshments for Christmas, and it was "up to me" to deliver the goods. I stood on one edge of the bed and took hold of the other with my hands, and, by throwing my weight back, attempted to turn it over. It was a hard struggle, and it seemed as if every time I would get it almost over a wave would wash it back. I kept this up for half an hour, all the time gradually floating down stream, until the wagon struck a sand-bar half a mile below. It stopped with a jerk, and, being numb with the cold, I lost my hold and went over backwards, taking one of the finest cold baths I ever had in my life. I went clear under, and, after floundering around in the water for some minutes weighted down by my heavy overcoat, I got straightened around and made for the shore. I then came back up the river, intending to go to a camp I had seen over on the hills while on my trip down. I found my horses had got out all right, but, like myself, were covered with ice and shivering with the cold. I tied up the harness, and, with my horses following, set out on a run for the camp, which was nearly a half-mile back and a short distance from the river; but instead of finding a nice warm fire awaiting me, I found the camp deserted and nothing but green wood to build a fire. It was a gloomy outlook, but I hunted around and found a rotten stump, from the inside of which I secured some dry, rotten wood. With this for kindling, I worked like a beaver, and finally got a fire started, but it was the slowest burning fire I ever saw in my life. After a whole lot of shivering and wishing I were in a warmer place, I got pretty well warmed up and started back to get the balance of the wagon out of the river. Of course, if I hadn't been going for whisky, this trouble wouldn't have happened; but if I hadn't been going for whisky, I wouldn't have cared whether I ever got the old wagon out or not. It is needless to add that I got the wagon out, resumed my journey to Paliponte, purchased the necessary refreshments and eatables, and returned home safe and sound. When I told my troubles, the boys gave me the laugh right, and that night there was much good-natured repartee over the hot toddy.

A few days after my unceremonious ducking in the Brazos River, Budd Willot,[2] George Mulligan, and I started out to round up a bunch of wild cattle which was grazing regularly in a small prairie near the timber. There was a small, rocky hill close to their grazing quarters. These hills were called peaks, as they were high and steep, more like a large mound than a hill. We hid our horses and ascended to the top of this peak to watch for the cattle to come out to graze. While waiting, we noticed a lot of broken rock thrown between two large ones, and as this looked suspicious, we investigated. On taking out the broken stones, we found the skeleton of an Indian and the usual big gray rat that is always found in an Indian's grave. The Indian had been buried with his arrows and soldier buttons, but the rat had discovered his resting-place and was making a home of it. The Indian's teeth and finger-bones were so white and perfect that we took them with us for ornaments. As we came up to the top of the peak again we saw the wild cattle grazing quietly, and a little further on were some deer and wild turkey. We then mounted our horses and started after the cattle. As soon as we came into view, the cattle saw us and broke for the timber. We had a race to head them off, and a five-foot ditch lay between us and the point we had to reach in order to turn the cattle. We let out our horses as fast as they could gallop, but in jumping the ditch the horses all went down, and we were sent sprawling on the grass. Before we could get our horses up and mount, the cattle had the best of the race, and it was impossible to get between them and the timber; so we gave up for the day. As we were stoved up considerably, and not in any too good a humor, we concluded the Indian teeth and bones were a "hoodoo"; so we threw them away, and returned to the ranch empty-handed.

CHAPTER VI

Hunting Buffalo for Profit

At the end of the winter, I quit J. C. Loving's employ, and went into business for myself.[1] The business I engaged in was killing buffalo for their hides. Next to owning a ranch, hunting buffalo was the most profitable business on the frontier. The hides brought good prices, bulls being worth two dollars, cows one dollar and seventy-five cents, and calves one dollar and seventy-five cents. Besides, the tongues, properly salted and dried, were in demand at seventy-five cents each, and the mop, or growth of long hair on the head, fifteen cents a pound.

The first thing I did was to go to Jacksboro to purchase an outfit, which consisted of horses and wagon, guns, knives, provisions, etc. I hired four men in Jacksboro, but when I had everything ready to start, only two showed up. The other two were on a "toot"; so we left without them, after giving instructions for them to follow as soon as they got sober. About fifteen miles out of Jacksboro I struck my first camp, and waited for the two "jags" to catch up. There were all kinds of Indians prowling around, and I wanted to be as strong as possible before going further. About dark the first evening we were in the camp, one of my men came in with a hard-luck story of how they got "loaded" and "shot up" the town. About the time they were in the height of their glory, Bill Gilson, the city marshal, [2] thought he would put an end to it. As he started for them, they put the spurs to their horses and started to run past him, when he promptly unloaded his shotgun into them. The man who came to the camp was the only one who got away; and after hearing his story, I rode back to town to get the other one out of trouble and recover the horse, if there was enough horse left to recover. When I came in, they were still picking shot out of my man's hide, and I "squared" it with the marshal, and left the injured man in the doctor's care. Luckily for both man and horse, the marshal's gun was loaded with bird-shot only, and they were not seriously injured. I left instructions for my man to find the camp where I had determined to locate permanently, and, securing the horse which he had ridden, I returned to the temporary camp.

The next morning we broke camp, and pulled out for the Little Wichita River. While traveling across the prairie, about sixty-five miles from the nearest town, one of our wagon-wheels broke down. In those days of frontier life one had to be equal to all kinds of emergencies, and I lost no time in shooting a buffalo, whose green hide I cut into strips to make some false spokes for the broken wheel. We then cut out spokes from some black-jack trees growing near by. These we wrapped tightly with the green buffalo hide, and bound them in place with more buffalo hide. After the spokes were placed, we built a fire and dried the repaired wheel over it, making the buffalo binding as hard as a stone. It was a rather crude piece of work, but it answered the purpose, and carried us to the head of the Big Wichita, where we located our permanent camp.

Our location was right in the heart of the big-game country, and the whole prairie. as far as one could see, was covered with buffalo, deer. antelope, and turkey, while the creeks were alive with ducks. It was a regular garden to look upon, and promised to produce very big returns in the way of buffalo skins. Besides the game, there was plenty of wild horses and wild cattle. They were not branded, and probably had been running wild for many years. While in this camp, we had the finest time on earth, according to our ideas of a time, and would not have traded places with the wealthiest man in the country. I chose a spot in a big hackberry grove, right under a rocky bluff, for the camp. It was the prettiest as well as the most convenient camp I ever struck. Right beside it was a big water-hole, fed by a spring, which furnished an abundant water supply at all times. The hackberry grove was in reality a thicket of unusual denseness, and we cut into it, for quarters to live in, a smoke-house, and a stable. For our living place, we cut a place large enough for two rooms. We cut the trees off level with the ground, and when we had made room enough, we took green buffalo hides, and stretched and dried them. With these hides we made a roof and walls for the residence, stable, and smoke-house. It was very cosy and comfortable, with a floor of dried buffalo skins and a buffalo-skin carpet, and we had nothing to complain of. We regarded it as a palace, and it was the warmest and most attractive camp on the plains. I could kill all the game we wanted without going one hundred yards from camp, and then there was good fishing, too. Our calf barbeques and fish-fries would have made the mouth of a connoisseur water.

I could kill all the buffalo we could use in shooting distance of the camp, and we required from fifty to one hundred a day. After skinning the buffalo, we would lay the hides out to dry. At infrequent intervals I would have freight-wagons come out and haul them to Fort Griffin, where a firm by the name of Lee & Reynolds, running a Government supply-store, bought them up.[3] The transportation to market cost me twenty-five cents each.

We took the tongues out of the buffalo right after killing, as the ravens were thick and would attack the tongue soon after a buffalo fell. We then salted them down and smoked them. According to our tastes, these tongues were the finest eating on earth.

After a time the hides accumulated on my hands to such an extent that I wanted to get rid of them in a lump, so I sent word to the traders that I would take one dollar apiece on the stake-ground for all the hides I had. They accepted my offer on short notice, and cleared up my stake-ground. I had no trouble in keeping it clear at that price, and I made money fast. At that time buffalo-hunting was the most profitable business on the plains, and never before nor since have I made the money I did out of skinning buffalo.

One day my man who was injured by the marshal's shotgun while "shooting up" Jacksboro dropped into camp. He hadn't fully recovered, and was not able to work. All he could do was to eat, and after lying around for ten days, I overheard him making a proposition to two of the boys to steal a bunch of horses from Terrell Brothers, who camped about ten miles away. They talked the matter over fully during the night and laid all their plans. The Terrell Brothers were the first settlers at Fort Worth,[4] and were good friends of mine, so the next morning, without letting anyone know where I [was] going, I set out to warn them of the proposed raid on their horses. I told the Terrells to keep their horses tied up that night, and I would go back to the camp and fire the would-be thieves. In this I had a bigger job than I anticipated, for when I told them what I had done, and ordered them to get out, they became ugly. I meant business, however, and they soon found it out. I started out by knocking one down with a gun, and had to almost kill the other before they realized that I was running the camp, and was going to run it without their assistance. They finally left the camp, going towards the Terrells' camp.

I guess they changed their minds about the matter, for they never showed up at the Terrells' and we never heard of them afterwards. A few days later we received information that the Indians had killed three men in that vicinity, but none of the hunters ever took the trouble to look it up.

After I got rid of the two would-be horse-thieves, I had only one man left. His name was Charley Buckley, and he was a good fellow. With only two of us, we couldn't take care of more than thirty buffalo a day, which made a big reduction in my profits.

One morning I shot eleven of the beasts and one deer right close to camp. All were dead but one, and he was so badly wounded that we thought he would be good and dead by the time we skinned the others, so we left him until the last one. When we finally came up to him, he was lying quietly and to all appearances dead, but when we turned his head over in order to get his tongue and mop, he jumped as quick as lightning and caught my man in the groin, tossing him about twenty feet. I shot him twice before he could make another move; once in the lungs, which made him belch about a tubful of blood, and that settled him.

Buffalo-hunters always aim to hit a buffalo in the lungs, as it will then belch blood, and the rest of the herd will paw and bellow over the blood, instead of running away. This gives the hunter an opportunity of getting more of them.

As soon as I saw the buffalo was dead, I turned to Charley and found that his genital organs were completely torn out by the infuriated beast's horns. He was in a horrible condition and the nearest doctor was a hundred miles away. I didn't know what to do for him, and things looked pretty bad. I picked him up and carried him to camp, a half-mile away, all the time worrying, because I was afraid I could do nothing to save him. I would carry him about a hundred yards at a time and then go back for my gun, working in this way until I got him into camp. After making him as comfortable as possible, I took some buffalo bones out of the fire which we had been roasting for the marrow, which we used for butter; and it was very palatable. I took this marrow and a small piece of rosin and a piece of alum about the size of an egg and melted them all together, making a salve. Then came the hardest part of the task—sewing up the wound. I had no silk thread, and was in a quandary as to what I could substitute, when it occurred to me that there was some silk thread in the neck-band of my undershirt. This I unraveled and used in a big buckskin needle, the only one I had. The eye of the needle was so large that the thread would have gone through five or six times. After washing his wound out carefully, I gave him some strong coffee, as I had nothing else to give him; in fact, I was in a bad way to care for even an ordinary sick person, let alone perform an operation which would worry the most skillful surgeon. I hated to go to work on him, but I thought that was the only way to save his life. Every time the needle pierced his flesh his cries were heart-rending, and I would pinch the flesh in order to cause numbness, hoping to cause him less pain. I worked away until I sewed a piece on which had been torn entirely off, and then applied the salve and bandaged the wound. He suffered intensely and was in great misery, when the thought of trying

whisky on him came to my mind. I had a small jug, and succeeded in getting a lot of the stuff down him. In a few minutes
after he drank the whisky, he dropped off to sleep. I sat beside
him all night long, and every time he would waken I would have
a hot toddy ready for him. It was a night of great anxiety for me,
and I was glad when morning came. When he awoke, I examined
him and found that the piece I had sewed on the day before had
come off again. I was ready to give up all hope, as I felt that he
could not survive without medical attention. I was afraid to attempt to sew the piece on again, so I threw it away and sewed the
wound up the best I could. After applying the salve liberally, I
gave him hot toddies as fast as he could drink them. My treatment
was in liberal doses, what there was of it, and I kept him drunk
all day long. I believe it was the lonesomest day I ever put in
anywhere. There I sat all through the day with a man whom I
believed to be fatally injured, and not a soul stopping at the camp
whom I could send for assistance. I did all I could and wanted to
do more, but didn't know what to do or how to do it. It was a day
of suspense, but he pulled through somehow, and I felt encour-
aged. I kept up the hot toddy and the salve treatment, and in a
day or two he showed signs of improving. He kept on getting
better, and the wound began to heal. Well, to make a long story
short, he was up and doing my cooking at the end of the week,
and in two weeks was able to stake all the hides I could bring to
him. A short time later he was apparently as stout as ever and
went into the field with me, skinning buffalo with all his old-time
skill and enthusiasm.

Soon after Charley recovered, I started out one night to go
to Fort Belknap after the mail.[5] As fast mail service and rural
delivery were not even thought of at that time, it was a long time
between mails, and I had not heard from my folks back in Ohio
for over a month. As I was riding along close by a small stream
just after coming out of some foot-hills, I came upon a small band
of Indians. They were all making cigarettes, and did not see me.
I rode into a big ravine, the only hiding place, and took off my

coat for the purpose of covering my horses's head, so he wouldn't
smell the Indians and snort. An Indian has a sort of a wet-dog
odor which the horses don't like, and they invariably snort and
paw when an Indian comes within smelling distance. I could hear
the Indians coming, and if any one thinks I didn't keep as still as
the proverbial mouse, he doesn't know what it is to meet a band
of hostile Indians on the prairie, alone. They passed within
twenty feet of me without seeing me; but a dog that was following
them saw me, and growled. They all stopped, and it was one of
the trying times of my life when an Indian came back to within a
few feet of me; but, as all was still, he turned and joined the rest.
I thought he had discovered me, as he was so close I could see
him by the star-light. I could have killed him, and was sorely
tempted to do so, as I rode one of the finest horses that ever trod
the prairies; but I had no chance to get away. The dog still kept
growling, but they paid no further attention to him, and rode
away. I didn't get a full breath of air all the time I was in the
ravine, and it was like taking a weight off my lungs when the
Indians resumed their journey. After they were out of hearing, I
hurried to Fort Belknap, where I found welcome letters from
home. The return trip was made the following night without incident. We always traveled at night, as the Indians were too thick
to travel during the day with any degree of safety. At night they
could not see a traveler, and it was only by accident that one
would meet them. Then there was always a better chance to get
away, as the Indians, not being sure of the number in a party,
were likely to hesitate before rushing on to an attack.

Late one evening a fine, large herd of buffalo came down
the valley, and stopped right close to camp. I went out for the
purpose of wounding one, so the herd would remain where they
were through the night. When one of a herd of buffalo is wounded,
the rest will usually stay with it until it dies or they are driven
away. They were grazing in a mesquite flat close by, when I crept
up. I picked out a fine one, and shot him in the loins. He fell,
and could not rise; so I returned to camp, and dreamed that night

of the fine stand I would have the next morning. The buffalo were just where I had left them the night before, the wounded one lying still and, to all appearances, dead. I crept up the branch to get close to the herd before beginning the slaughter. I was armed with a big Creedmore gun that weighed eighteen pounds,[6] and two belts of cartridges, which, together with a six-shooter buckled on, loaded me down completely. As I passed the one I wounded the night before, he shook his head at me, as if he knew that I was the cause of his trouble. I thought I would keep him from making trouble, and shot him through the lungs. At the crack of the gun he was up and after me, and, as I was only about thirty feet away, I threw the gun and started to run for a big, deep ditch which was about fifty yards off. I did some pretty tall running, even if I was loaded down with cartridges, and only those who have been chased by a buffalo know how fast a man can run under similar conditions. The buffalo are big, awkward, clumsy animals, and look as if they couldn't run at all; but their appearance is deceiving, and they can get over ground faster than any man cares to run. When I reached the ditch, the buffalo was still about thirty feet behind me, with his head down and coming at full gallop. I drew my six-shooter, thinking to shoot him in the loins, so he couldn't run, as that is the only place a light gun or revolver has any effect on them. To shoot a buffalo in the head with a revolver is just like shooting at a stone-wall; that is, it has just about as much effect. Just then the pursuing buffalo stopped suddenly, and belched up a lot of blood. I knew then he was gone, and it gave me much satisfaction to see him topple over, dead. The shot I had given him the night before was considered sure death by all buffalo-hunters; consequently I did not use the usual precautions in approaching him in the morning. When I made sure he was dead, I returned and got my gun, and then laid down for a good rest. I hadn't disturbed the big herd, and they were grazing as quietly as if nothing had happened. However, I thought one experience with a wounded buffalo was enough for one day; so I returned to camp.

When I reached there, I found three freight-wagons after my hides, and four "nester" wagons after a winter supply of buffalo meat. In those days the farmers who came out to the frontier and settled down to farming were called "nesters." They were all loaded with provisions and what the frontiersman loves best on earth—whisky. After a few introductory remarks, they produced the whisky, and then a few hours were spent over a "social glass." We entertained them royally, with a dinner of the best the plains provided, and, after relating my morning's experience, they were anxious to kill some buffalo, so I invited them to stay over until the next day, when I intended to make another killing, and they could have a chance. There was too much good red liquor in camp to hunt buffalo or do anything but justice to that, for the rest of the day. We sat around the camp-fire all day and until late in the evening, swapping lies and getting better acquainted with each other, through the medium of hot toddies.

Next morning I saddled my horse and rode up on the divide to reconnoiter, while they were getting breakfast. I saw a big herd grazing in toward the bluff, so I went back to camp and told the boys to hitch up and drive to a point about two miles out on the ridge, and to wait there one hour, in order to give me time to make a stand before they came into view, as they might frighten the buffalo.

By this time I had entirely recovered from the little scare of the previous day, and, with a small flask of "corn-juice" in my pocket, set out to make a stand on the herd. They were just coming into a pool of water under the cliff when I came up. I climbed up to the top of the cliff and waited until they had all drunk plenty, and were turning away. I then started to work, shooting them down as fast as I could fire. On account of being on an elevated position, I could not give them a dead shot, as by shooting downward it was impossible to reach the vital spots, the lungs or heart. I did the next best thing, and aimed at their loins. It was not long until I had thirty-seven of the animals down, but only two were dead. As they were all shot through the loins, they were perfectly helpless, but with plenty of life and rage left. I thought thirty-seven would give the "nesters" plenty of sport, so I went back to the point where they were waiting and told them to come on. I told them what I had done, and warned them in regard to the danger of being attacked by a wounded buffalo. They were much pleased with the opportunity of engaging in a hand-to-hand encounter with the monarchs of the plains, and the fact that they had to be shot the second time promised to be great sport for them. They commenced getting their guns ready before we were within a half-mile of the buffalo, and pretended to be very brave and cautious. Near the top of a cliff we had a lunch, before starting in to finish the work. The lunch consisted of dried tongue, bread, and whisky—principally whisky. After we got pretty well "loaded," I took them to the top of the bluff and showed them the buffalo. Some were lying down and some were sitting on their haunches. Again I warned them of the danger they were about to face, but they were still brave and anxious to get down among them. I told them to go ahead, while Charley and I stayed on top of the cliff to watch the fun which we knew would be sure to come when greenhorns attempted to shoot buffalo. They were armed with old-fashioned muzzle-loading rifles, which were all right for squirrels, but just a little light for buffalo. How we laughed, as they crept down with more caution than an old Indian-fighter surprising a band of Commanches! When they got up to the wounded buffalo, they opened fire, shooting right and left, with about as much effect as if their guns were loaded with peas. They gained courage with every step, and were soon right into the bunch. Every time a buffalo was hit he would only have to shake his head or bat his eye to give the "nesters" a fright.

Occasionally one would get up on his haunches with an effort that looked as if he were coming right after them; then they would cut and run for dear life, leaving behind hats and everything else that was loose. The would-be hunters got so excited at this work that they would often forget to ram a bullet down after the powder, all of which furnished us with more amusement than we had enjoyed in many days.

After tiring themselves out and failing to kill any buffalo, I went down with my big gun and completed the job. The grangers loaded their wagons with meat and we returned to camp. That night we held another carnival with John Barleycorn and frontier delicacies.

We spent the evening as all such evenings are spent— fighting the battles over between drinks. The next evening the freighters and grangers began to get ready to return to the Fort. They had a boy with them, about thirteen or fourteen years of age, and he trembled every time anyone mentioned Indians. I had built a small fort out of the rocks, on top of the bluff beside the camp, for protection in the event of an Indian raid. From this fort one could see the country for miles in every direction, and three or four men could have held it against a whole tribe of Indians. As soon as he had his breakfast, the boy climbed the steps which I had dug out of the cliff to this fort, and took his position, on the look-out for Indians. He had spent the afternoon before watching for the approach of redskins, but the fact that they did not appear didn't seem to quiet his nerves any. About 11 o'clock, as we were getting dinner and making merry in camp, the boy yelled to us excitedly, "Here comes a lot of men on horseback. I think they are Indians, as they look awful funny. Hurry! come quick!" We all jumped at once, and from a happy camp scene everything changed in a second to one of excitement and turmoil. The grang- ers were so scared that they didn't know what they were doing, and fluttered around like a lot of chickens attacked by a hawk. They were tying their horses, getting their guns, hunting their powder-horns and cap-boxes all at once, and the air was full of "Oh, my poor wife!" "What will become of us if the Indians get after us?" and similar expressions, which showed how frightened they were. The men with the freight-wagons were not worried about such little things as Indian attacks, when they were prepared for them, and, like myself, took things easy. There were fifty-one long steps up to the fort, and I climbed up to see what the Indians were doing. When I reached the fort, here came the grangers after me, completely winded and puffing like engines under a full head of steam.

Sure enough, there were the Indians, coming down a long slope on the trail the freighters and "nesters" made in reaching the camp. The little fort would hold but four men comfortably, and they all wanted into it. I ordered them all to lie down except two men and the boy, who crowded into the fort with me and Charley. Charley by this time had become thoroughly hardened to frontier life, and was a valuable man. The Indians were slowly coming down the wagon trail. They had to cross a large flat before reaching the Wichita River, and, as our camp was on the opposite side of the river, there was no danger from an immediate attack.

I sent several of the men down to the camp to bring up all the guns and ammunition, together with a supply of water and provisions, so that we would be prepared if the Indians besieged us. I had three thousand cartridges for my big Creedmore and plenty of ammunition for the smaller guns. I did not feel alarmed, as I could have killed every Indian in the bunch before they could possibly have reached the fort; but the strength of our position wasn't appreciated by the grangers, who became more frightened every minute. When the Indians were about a mile away, I said to the boys: "I'll just send them a feeler, to see how they like my Creedmore gun." They were riding along single file, and, knowing the range of my gun, I was certain of getting pretty close to them. When I fired, they could not hear the report, as the wind was against them, and the smoke had faded away before they saw it. The shot struck close, and surprised them. They all huddled up together, and tried to locate its source. Just for luck, I sent two more shots after them, and, thinking I had aimed too low the first time, I elevated my rifle for the second and third shots. The bullets must have whistled over their heads, and they located me.

They were surprised that I could reach them at that distance, and lit out for a mesquite thicket a short distance away. We kept watch until dark, when I put out pickets to prevent their surprising us, and prepared to break camp that night. I loaded two wagons with hides and two with buffalo tongues. The "nester" wagons were all loaded with meat for the coming winter; so we pulled out, leaving sixty-three buffalo hides staked out. We drove thirty-five miles that night, to the round timber on the Brazos River, where we stopped and rested our horses all the next day. The following morning I sent my tongues to Graham City and Fort Jacksboro.[7] There were a good many soldiers at these points, and they liked buffalo tongues; so I had no trouble in disposing of my supply at fifty and seventy-five cents apiece. When I had sold out, I was loaded down with one- and two-dollar bills and shinplasters.

Although buffalo-hunting is very profitable, and I quit away "ahead of the game," it got tiresome toward the last, and I longed for a change. With only one man, I could not cope with the Indians, so I began to look around for other fields to conquer.

CHAPTER VII

With the Rangers

From Fort Jacksboro I went to Fort Griffin, and sold my buffalo-hunting outfit. From there I went up to Loving's ranch, in the Big Loss Valley, where I learned a big company of Texas Rangers, under Captain Hamilton, was camped. Ranger life looked pretty good to me, as there was forty dollars per month in it and plenty of plunder. So I applied to Captain Hamilton for admission into his company, and, as I was a large, stout, able-bodied man, with a good gun and a better horse, he was glad to accept me.[1] The Rangers were camped in the valley near the ranch, and were scouting the country for Indians.

There was always something doing with the Rangers, and we kept the Indians busy keeping out of our way. One day we started out for a scouting trip up the Wichita, and struck a fresh trail. The band numbered thirty-five, and they had evidently just come in from the Reservation. We took up the trail and followed it all day. At dark we stopped to rest our horses and eat a lunch. After a short rest, we saddled up and took the trail again. The grass was tall and damp, and we could follow the trail as well at night as by day. We were in the saddle all night and by twelve o'clock the next day reached the Cox Mountains, where the great massacre had occurred, about eighteen months before. The Government supply-train on the way to Fort Griffin, in charge of a detachment of soldiers, was surrounded by Indians. Only one man escaped, the rest being massacred and the wagons burned.[2]

The trail led up the side of the mountains, and we began the ascent. When we were about half way up, we saw two Indians coming toward us. They wore red blankets, and acted as if they hadn't seen us, until they came to within three hundred yards of our party. Then they suddenly looked up, and turned quickly and ran for a big gap in the mountains, which narrowed down to a cow-trail just wide enough for one cow to pass. The Indians played their part well, and though we supposed it was a ruse to lead us into a trap, we knew there were only thirty-five in the band we were following, and did not fear that number, so we

gave chase. There were twenty-nine in our party, including Adjt.-
Gen. Jones, of Texas,[3] and Tom Wilson, sheriff of Paliponte
County.[4] We pulled right in after the two Indians, following the
trail until we come to a big washout which had formed a basin.
In this basin were concealed two hundred Indians, under the lead-
ership of Big Tree and Satanta,[5] where we expected to find only
thirty-five. We rode up to within a hundred and fifty yards of them
before we discovered that the original band had joined another
and larger bunch. We has just discovered their presence when
they opened fire, and eleven of our horses went down and three
men were wounded. One had his left arm shot away, another was
wounded in the leg, while the third received a shot in the back.
We charged the Indians, and succeeded in stampeding them,
much to the consternation of the two big chiefs, who ran in front
of them waving their blankets, in an endeavor to stop the band.
When they got about five hundred yards away, Big Tree and Satanta, who had taken in the situation at a glance, and knew they
had a tremendous advantage over us with eleven of our horses
gone, stopped the stampede. We realized fully the trouble we had
gotten into when Satanta and Big Tree had their men lined up
again; so we sought cover in a deep ditch, formed by washouts,
which ran through a small grove of big trees. We tied our horses,
and brought Billy Glass, who was wounded in the back, and the
fellow who was wounded in the leg, whose name I don't remember,[6] into the ravine with us, to keep them from being scalped.

By this time the Indians were coming for us at full gallop.
John Cone, whose arm was badly shot up, ran to the creek and
dived into a water pool to hide.[7] Tom Wilson was also cut off
from joining us, and took a position behind a big oak tree. Another one of the boys, who had emptied his gun into the advancing Indians, was cut off, too, and he started down the creek with
two Indians after him. He snapped his gun at them time after
time, in an effort to check their pursuit; but they followed right
after him with drawn lances, until he came to the waterhole
where Cone was hiding, when he threw his gun at the Indians,

and leaped into the pool. Cone, thinking he was an Indian, took a shot at him, but missed, and the Indians gave up the fight and joined the main band.

The Indians rode pell-mell right up to the ditch, and jumped their horses over our heads. This was our opportunity, and we made the best of it, shooting them as fast as we could fire while they were jumping the ditch. After they had all crossed, we had about thirty of their number down. Some were in the ditch, and some fell after they crossed. It taught them a lesson in regard to charging us, so they withdrew to a small rocky peak about three hundred yards distant from the top of which they could pick off every one in the ditch at the point where we were located. We moved farther down, to a more protected location, and they kept up a steady fire from the top of the peak, in a vain effort to dislodge us. Sheriff Wilson, who had still held his position behind the oak tree, tried several times to join us, but every time he would stick his head out a bullet from an Indian rifle would chip the bark too close for comfort.

In order to keep the Indians busy, we would push our hats up on the bank, and they would shoot them off instantly.

Billy Glass soon began to suffer for water, and, as he was mortally wounded, Ed Bailey and Knox Glass, a brother of the wounded man, volunteered to go to the creek and get it.[8] It was all a man's life was worth to show his head, let alone go for water, but, as they rode racing horses, they stood a better show than the rest of the boys. The nearest point in the stream where they had to go for water was about three hundred yards distant, and the peak, where the Indians had taken up their position was about the same distance, only a little farther up. Bailey and Knox Glass took three canteens, and made a run for the trees where we had our horses tied. They mounted their fleet-footed racers, and reached the creek in double-quick time. The Indians, seeing their move, started in to cut off their retreat, and we kept a steady fire on the leaders to hold them back. Bailey was down by the water's edge and succeeded in filling two canteens before the Indians got a good start. Glass, seeing that they would have to hurry to keep from being cut off, said: "Come on, Ed; they are coming, and will cut us off." "No; I will fill this one, if they do catch me," was Bailey's reply. He did fill it, and mounted his horse. Glass was off like a flash, and made the ditch where we were entrenched easily; but Bailey failed to take advantage of his horses's fleetness, and was the victim of the most horrible butchery I ever witnessed.

Instead of letting his horse out as Glass did, Bailey seemed confused, and held him in. His horse was exceptionally fast, and, with the bad start, he had a chance to make it; but he did not head straight for the ditch, and in a few seconds the Indians had him cut off. They closed in on him, driving him around in a circle, all the time shooting arrows into him and yelling with fiendish glee. We were powerless to come to his rescue, as the only way we could cope with such a large body of Indians was by fighting them from cover. Our ammunition was running low, and only eighty rounds of cartridges remained, when the adjutant-general ordered us to cease firing. He saw that saving Bailey was out of the question, and it was absolutely necessary that we reserve our ammunition, in the event of a charge from the main body of Indians, which was likely to take place at any time.

After shooting seventeen arrows into Bailey's back, they rode up and pulled him from his horse. Then we were compelled to witness the most revolting sight of our lives. They held Bailey up in full view, and cut him up, and ate him alive. They started by cutting off his nose and ears; then hands and arms. As fast as a piece was cut off, they would grab it, and eat it as ravenously as the most voracious wild beast.

We were all hardened to rough life, and daily witnessed scenes that would make a "tenderfoot's" blood run cold; but to see Ed Bailey die by inches and eaten piecemeal by the blood-thirsty Comanches and Kiowas made our hearts quail. We could see the blood running from their mouths as they munched the still quivering flesh. They would bat their eyes and lick their mouths after every mouthful. The effect of these disgusting movements on us was but to increase our desire for revenge, and we often had it later on. After eating all the fleshy parts of our brave comrade, they left him lying where they had captured him, and returned to the peak. The Indians remained on the peak or behind it until dark, and we spent the rest of the afternoon in the ditch, but keeping a good lookout. We had ceased firing, as Adjt.-Gen. Jones' orders were not to fire until they were within fifty yards of us, so we could secure the ammunition of the dead or wounded Indians. However, none came that near; but there were plenty of dead ones on all sides, that we had killed before our ammunition ran low.

Along in the evening Billy Glass died, the Indian bullet having penetrated his stomach and lungs. About 8 o'clock we took the remains of Glass, and struck out for Fort Jacksboro, twenty-five miles away, to get reinforcements from the soldiers quartered there. As soon as we were well on the road, and felt safe from pursuit, we dug a grave and buried Glass. There was a lot of colored troops at Fort Jacksboro, and the officers detailed two hundred of them to return with us and put the Indians to rout. They made so much noise while on the march that we could not hope to surprise the Indians. An Indian could have heard those darkies singing and laughing a mile away, but they furnished us with plenty of amusement on the way. When we neared the battlefield, we struck camp until daylight. We had all kinds of trouble in keeping the "niggers" quiet, as they would rather have frightened the Indians away by their noise than have defeated them in battle. One big black, who was blacker than the ace of spades, refused to take his post on the picket-line; so they hung him up by the thumbs to a convenient oak tree, and left him there for four hours. At daybreak we rode over to the scene of our encounter of the day before, but there was not an Indian in sight. We first gathered up the remains of Ed Bailey for burial. Nothing but the skeleton and the internal organs remained, as the Indians had eaten all the meat off the bones.[9]

After burying Bailey, we tried to locate the Indians. Although the ground was strewn with bodies the day before, they had gathered up all their dead and wounded, and made off. We struck their trail, leading to Fort Sill, but the colored soldiers wouldn't follow it,[10] and, after looking around awhile, we returned to Fort Jacksboro.[11]

Big Tree and Satanta, the big chiefs of the band, were afterward captured and sent to prison by the officers at Fort Sill.[12]

Another adventure, that is worth recording here, took place just one month from the day we had the fight in the ditch.[13] The moon was full, and the Indians full of deviltry, so we went out on a scouting trip, hoping we might run across some marauding parties. We stopped near the place of our former fight, and, looking across the valley, saw seven Indians on the other side, headed directly toward us. We fell back into the timber, and awaited their coming. They stopped at a creek about a mile away, and watered their horses. They stood there for some time, and then came out of the creek single file, and started for the timber where we were hidden. From the direction they were coming, we estimated that they would strike the timber where there was a high bench about a hundred feet back from the edge of the prairie. We hid ourselves accordingly.

Finally they came along, whittling out dog-wood arrows, and chatting together. They entered the timber just where we wanted them to, when we rushed out, and fell in behind them, cutting off their retreat. As there was the high bench in front of them, and we were behind them, they couldn't get away. Only about half of our company of Rangers was present, the other half being down with the measles, and the rest of the company was made up of an escort from another company, under Lieut. Long.[14] We were armed with the new 45-caliber Colt's revolvers and new carbine needle-guns. We had received them only a few days before, and they were a great improvement over our old cap-and-ball navies and Spencer and Henry rifles. They were up-to-

With the Rangers 55

date weapons, and the carbine rifle is even to-day the best gun for general use.

They hadn't heard us fall in behind them, and they kept on in single file until they came to the bench, when we made a rush on them. They were taken by surprise, and started to run, when Lieut. Long pulled his six-shooter and fired the first shot. He caught an Indian in the back and uncoupled him. There were two deep ditches, which formed a "V," having been washed out in that shape by heavy rains; so wide that they couldn't jump them at night, and they were compelled to turn and meet us. There were five bucks, a squaw, and a renegade white man in the party. We all opened fire on them, but, as the timber was thick, our fire wasn't as effective as it would have been under other conditions. Three of the bucks went down, when the squaw went into action. She emptied two six-shooters at us, but none of the shots took effect. Then, jumping from her horse, she clasped her hands on her breast, shouting, "Me squaw, me squaw," thinking she would get off because she was a woman.[15] Someone shot her in the stomach, as a squaw horsethief wasn't considered any better than a buck horsethief, and she walked over and sat down by a tree. Lieut. Long became engaged in a hand-to-hand encounter with the chief of the Indian raiders, after each had emptied his gun. They clinched and were struggling on the ground when we came up. The lieutenant was a big, powerful man and so was the Indian. We put our guns to the Indian's head and asked him if he would surrender. "No, you heap Tahones (Texas) s—— — b——," said the Indian in reply; and we fired, shooting his head clear off. Only a small piece of his skull remained, and that stuck to the back of his neck.[16] That made five down.

One Indian, who was riding a little mare which he had stolen from Loving, discovered an opening around the ditch and went through, making his escape. We sent a shower of bullets after him, but he was riding like lightning, and we never knew whether we hit him or not.[17]

The renegade was the only one left, and he got a half mile away before we got him. We killed his horse first, and he got behind the dead animal, lying there with his gun cocked, but he did not fire a shot. We couldn't understand why he didn't shoot at us, as a renegade receives less quarter than an Indian when captured. He bobbed his head up and down behind the horse so we couldn't get a shot at him. We dismounted and crept up to some trees a short distance from the spot, and took turn about in shooting at his head every time it would appear above the horse's body. Finally one of the boys caught him between the eyes, and the renegade's raiding days were over. The bullet tore off the top of his head, and he was dead before we reached him. On examination, we found that he had been shot through twice before we had killed his horse, which accounted for his strange actions. He was apparently bewildered and so could not shoot us.

We went back to where the Indians lay, and found the squaw still alive, nursing her wound in the stomach. Another well-aimed shot put an end to her; then we proceeded to skin them. I skinned the squaw, taking only the skin from the body proper, leaving the arms, neck, and legs. We tanned these Indian hides afterwards, and I made a purse out of the squaw's belly. The boys made quirts (a kind of a braided riding-whip) out of the bucks' hides.[18]

From the Big Loss Valley we moved to Flattop Mountain, on Salt Creek Prairie, where we camped nearly two months. There was good water here, and Flattop Mountain afforded an excellent view to watch the movements of the Indians. The time passed quietly while we were camped here, and we didn't hear of any Indian depredations anywhere. One day, while some of the boys were grazing their horses near the scene of the massacre of the Government mule-train, they found an Indian grave in a pile of rock, and dug it out. The Indian had evidently been buried many years, as the bones of the skeleton were whitened and showed marks of age. In the grave, behind the body, they found two ladies' gold breastpins, a gold ring, a butcher-knife, several strings of beads, a soldier's overcoat, bow and arrow, and five six-shooters. The six-shooters were well greased with tallow, to keep them from rusting, and one of them had been fired off once. It was the custom among the Indians to bury a brave's earthly possessions with him, and, as they were continually raiding the settlements, stealing everything that was of value, there was almost always enough in a grave to pay for digging it up. The boys on the frontier never failed to rifle an Indian's grave every time they found one.

From Flattop Mountain we moved to a point on the Brazos River near the round timber, where we camped about two months. During a rainy season, while we were camped here, the Indians came down the river. We struck the trail of a large band, and started to run them down. It had rained hard every day for several days, and the Brazos River was full nearly to overflowing; so we rode down the river a little way, for the best place to swim it. On the other side we took up the trail again, and followed it for some distance, until it led into a mesquite flat. The prairie was so soft that our horses had difficulty in getting over it, which necessarily made our pursuit slow. We hunted the flat over for Indians, but we found only one, a squaw, who was the wife of old Black Crow.[19] It seemed that Black Crow was in the habit of beating his wife, just as some of his civilized white brothers do, and on this occasion he had beaten her and driven her back. She was resting in the mesquite flat when we found her, and when she saw us, she tied her pony to a mesquite tree and threw her arms and legs around another, holding on with all her strength. We broke he hold, and took her along to camp. We kept her with us for two months, when Black Crow, learning where she was, appealed to the officers at Fort Sill, who furnished him with a squad of soldiers to come out to our camp and get her. During her stay in camp she appeared to be quite contented, especially as we kept her in the commissary, where she could eat all the sugar she wanted. She had a woman's sweet tooth, and went after the sugar just the same as a society girl after chocolates and bon-bons, eating as high as a quart during the night. She was also cleanly

in her habits, which is more than can be said of the average
squaw, and would go to the creek and wash herself three times a
day. When Black Crow and the soldiers came and demanded her
release, she did not want to go with them. She kicked, and
scratched, and bit, when Black Crow took hold of her to force
her to return to his bed and board; but when she saw he wouldn't
return without her, she gave up the struggle and went along. It
was not recorded whether Black Crow gave her regular beatings
after that or not, but they are still living together on Cash [Cache]
Creek, near Lawton, Oklahoma.

Occasionally a man comes out to the frontier full of bravery
and braggadocio, and we picked up such a man for the company.
He was from Arkansas, and what he hadn't done, and what he
wouldn't do in Texas, were too trivial for consideration. We
tested his courage one night, and found it just what we expected,
a little yellow. To keep the Indians from stampeding the horses,
we drove them into the corral every night, and took turn about in
guarding them. When it came Ark's turn, as we called him, he
wasn't quite so enthusiastic, but took his place at the proper time.
We had a bear skin in camp, and a fellow named Yarborough[20]
got it out, and tied a lariat to it, leaving it alongside the corral,
then with the other end of the lariat secreted himself along the
bank of the creek running by the camp. He pulled this bear hide
along the ground past the corral, and it made the horses frantic.
They snorted and reared and plunged, while Ark only hit the high
places between the corral and camp, yelling "Indians!" at the top
of his voice with every jump. We were all "on," and, grabbing
our guns, rushed out to carry out our part of the programme. Of
course we searched the premises, but found nothing. In the meantime Yarborough had pulled the bear hide down into the creek.
and, as there was nothing doing, we assured Ark that he had
nothing to fear, pulled the bear skin to the opposite side of the
corral again, and went back to the camp. After giving Ark a few
minutes to quiet his nerves, Yarborough pulled on the bear skin
again. When Ark saw the big black bear thing crawling around

the corral toward him, and the horses in a tempest, he was frightened worse than before, and, letting out a yell that awoke the prairie for miles around, he made the distance from the corral to camp in record-breaking time. We all went out again, and this time found the bear hide which was the cause of Ark's trouble. We "jollied" him about allowing such a little thing to frighten him; then he got mad and threatened vengeance. Next morning he found out in some way that Yarborough was the man who manipulated the rope, and promptly challenged him to fight a duel. It was an affair of honor, and the gentleman from the Ozarks did not enjoy having his honor trampled upon. Yarborough just as promptly accepted his challenge, and it was agreed that the management of the affair should be placed in the hands of Captain Hamilton. We were all "in on the deal," and the arrangements were made with all the solemnity of the real thing.

Eleven o'clock that morning was the time scheduled for the duel to be fought, and Ark carefully watched every move that was made until time was called. A few minutes before the appointed hour we assembled on a nice grassy plot alongside the creek, and lined up with six-shooters in hand. The captain took his position in front of us, and called to both men to step forward. The captain, having the loading of the pistols, had extracted the bullets from six cartridges, and loaded each weapon with three blanks. He instructed them as follows: "Stand with your backs to each other, holding the guns down by the side; step off fifteen paces, and, at the count of 'three,' wheel and fire." In handing them the guns, the captain took good care to keep them pointed downward, so they couldn't see that they were not loaded. They took their positions, and the captain ordered, "March!" They stepped off fifteen paces each, and were standing with their backs to each other, when the captain began to count slowly, with a deep, resonant voice, which sounded very solemn indeed. The stillness was oppressive. When the count began, "One," Ark showed signs of nervousness—the oppressive stillness was telling on him; "Two," and Ark first turned his head, then turned clear around, and, in a whipped-dog tone, said: "Gentlemen, I weaken." Just then the captain yelled, "Three!" and Yarborough wheeled and fired. The brave gentleman from Arkansas dropped his gun, and hit the prairie with the speed of a jack-rabbit. Yarborough was right after him, but he couldn't have been caught with a locomotive. He made straight for the settlements, and we were afterwards informed that he never stopped until he reached Arkansas. He left a good horse and eighty dollars pay coming.

Yarborough was afterward appointed marshal of Albuquerque, New Mexico; but he was too handy with his six-shooter, and, after killing two men, was hanged.[21]

CHAPTER VIII

Weeding out the Outlaws

Our next orders were to go to Fort Griffin, and from there proceed against the outlaws who were making the frontier of Texas their temporary home. At this time Texas was the Mecca for criminals driven out of other States, and, except for the Texas Rangers, they were out of reach of the law. If a man had committed robbery or murder in Ohio, Illinois, or any settled State, and it wasn't safe for him where officers of the law could reach him, he made a bee-line for Texas. On the frontier they would hunt buffalo and work on the ranches without fear of molestation, as no officer from the cities or counties of other States would undertake to follow a man through the hostile Indian country. This class of criminals were becoming very thick in Texas, and the authorities were besieged with appeals from State, county, and city officials all over the country to arrest the fugitives. At Fort Griffin we were loaded with warrants, and then proceeded to the buffalo-grounds to execute them. The first month we arrested one hundred and two men who were wanted for crimes in other States, and delivered them up to the forts, to await the arrival of officers.[1] After cleaning up the buffalo-grounds, we were ordered to go to Montague County to effect the arrest of culprits named Cribbs and Preston, and the Brown brothers, who had murdered the Meeks family. The brush was so thick that the sheriff and his deputies had about given up hope of capturing them. There were so many hiding-places that the criminals had no trouble in eluding the sheriff's party, but they found they were "up against" a different proposition when they had the Rangers to deal with. When we reached the vicinity where the fugitives were supposed to be hiding, we camped around in the brush, and in a short time succeeded in capturing all four.[2] We took our prisoners to Gainesville, which had a better jail than Montague, as the sheriff was afraid of a lynching.[3] They were afterwards tried in Gainesville on a change of venue, convicted of murder, and hanged.[4]

The day we left Gainesville, we got to sampling the whisky

on tap at the various bars, and found it so much to our liking that
we each took a quart bottle along. The result of it was that we
got good and drunk before we got out of town. Sheriff Perkins of
Montague County,[5] was with us, and he took a turn at "shooting
up" the town. After he had finished this innocent bit of entertainment, we saddled our horses, and set out for Montague, each man
carrying his quart of whisky in his saddle-pocket. While riding
over the trail two abreast, the sheriff and the captain in the lead,
a little puff of wind blew the sheriff's hat off. I was riding next
behind the sheriff, and when his hat blew off, I pulled my gun
and shot a hole in it. The rest of the boys did the same; but the
sheriff didn't like it, and was hot all the way through. The captain, however, laughed at him and "jollied" him until he cooled
off. We hadn't gone far until the captain's hat blew off, and it was
treated in the same way. That started the ball rolling, and it ended
in every one's having his hat shot full of holes. One of the party
wouldn't "stand for it," and struck out across the prairie. He was
riding a good horse, and we chased him three miles before we
caught him, and threw his hat up in the air, riddling it with bullets. We were now all hatless, and had an all-day ride through the
hot sun before we could reach Montague. We made the best of
the situation, however, and laughed and joked our troubles away.
We rode into Montague hatless, but proceeded at once in search
of something that would answer the purpose. That was all we
found, too, as there were only two hats in the town of the style
we wore; and we were compelled to buy some small, white, cot-
ton hats until we could reach another town and find what we
wanted.

From Montague we rode back to Fort Griffin, where the
local vigilance committee was making trouble.[6] Here we found
hats that we felt right in. The vigilance committee had been running things with a high hand, in hanging men without trial, and
before they got through they had a split-up in their ranks. The
two factions then organized two separate committees, one calling
themselves Moderators, and the other Regulators. The Modera-

tors protested against hanging a man without trial or investigation to determine whether he was guilty or not, while the Regulators wanted to hang every man who could not give a good account of himself. The result was a bitter war between the two committees, and they got to killing each other.[7] Johnny Long, ex-sheriff of Shackelford County,[8] was one of the leading Moderators, and, being a dangerous man in a row, the Regulators determined to get rid of him. They had him arrested and placed in an improvised jail and chained down with nine other prisoners. During the night someone, supposed to be a Regulator, got into the lockup and shot and killed him.[9] Long was a friend of Bill Gilson, the marshal, and Gilson hunted me up and told me the whole story. I got him a new suit of clothes and took him down to the river bank. There I had him change clothes, and, after shooting his hat and clothes, scattered them along the bank, so as to indicate that he was murdered and his body thrown into the river. By this time the Regulators got wind of the fact that Gilson had given them away, and they started out to hunt for him. They didn't search long until they found his clothes. They were suspicious of being tricked, and, before taking any action, all the members got together and compared notes. It developed that none of them had killed him, and they continued their search. We had a pretty good start by this time, as I put Gilson on a big State mule and we rode all night, reaching the Brazos River in the Fish Creek Mountains before halting. Gilson was a hard drinker and got the "jim-jams" on my hands. I took him to an old friend who was camped down on the Fish Creek Mountains. I swam my horse across the river and rode over to Fort Belknap, where I bought some whisky for him, and returned. As soon as he got a little whisky into him, he was all right; so I went back to camp and picked up a few of the boys. We returned and got Gilson, taking him to Austin, where he told the State authorities all about the workings of the rival vigilance committees at Fort Griffin.[10] The officials were very much worked up over it, and issued warrants for the arrest of the whole outfit. We went back to Fort Griffin and arrested them all.

They furnished bail and went down to Austin to "square it" with the authorities. It cost them about $50,000 to get out of the scrape, and that broke up the vigilance business at Fort Griffin.[11]

We were then ordered to arrest Sam Bass and his band of Union Pacific train-robbers, who were making the frontier their home for the present.[12] We located them in a cedar brake on Iron-eye Creek, in Paliponte County.[13] We entered the brake, but they gave us the slip and got away.[14] We didn't like hunting white men, so didn't follow them any farther, but returned to camp. Captain Hamilton quit the company[15] and many of the boys followed suit. I was left in charge, and decided to disband the company; so I took all of the outfit which belonged to the State to Thorp Spring, where I turned it over to June Peak, who was organizing a new company at Dallas, to hunt Sam Bass and the other Union Pacific train-robbers.[16] We disbanded here, and the boys who had remained with me went home.

CHAPTER IX

Running a Saloon in Texas

While I was with the Rangers, my chum and bunk-mate was
N. F. Lock, and when Company B disbanded, we remained together.[1] We were undecided as to what to do for the future, and
went to Fort Belknap in search of almost any old kind of an opening. There was no saloon there, and, for want of something better
to do, we opened up one. I tended bar and managed the saloon,
while my partner found employment as a clerk in a general store.
The saloon business proved a good venture, as business was
lively and money plenty. Everything was 25 cents a drink, as
silver quarters and 25-cent shinplasters were the smallest denominations in circulation. No two-for-a-quarter drinks "went,"
and nobody expected it.[2]

Millet Brothers had a large cattle ranch near the Fort, and
employed a large number of "punchers." They were a tough lot,
too, as Millet Brothers would not hire a man unless he was a
fighter.[3] They did a lot of shady work, and needed good men to
execute their plans in raiding the ranges for stray cattle. The men
from Millet Brothers' ranch were regular patrons at our bar, and
they would come in in bunches of from twenty-five to fifty. The
first place they headed for on reaching Fort Belknap was the bar,
where they would all line up and drink round after round of frontier whisky. At this stage I would begin watering the whisky, and
gradually get it so weak that it would hardly be recognized as
whisky. I did this in order to keep them from getting too full. I
would also manage to collect about twice for every round. One
man would order the drinks and pay for the same, and then I
would go to the other end of the bar and pick out another fellow,
saying that the last round of drinks was on him. They never
"tumbled," and always had plenty of money. By giving them
watered whisky, it would not be long until they were all right
again, and ready to start in over again. By keeping this up all
afternoon, or all evening, I would have a nice little sum of money
to show for my day's business.

One night Charley Roberts brought a crowd of his men in

and lined up at the bar. By 11 o'clock they were all "loaded," and, as there were no other customers in the saloon, I decided to close up, as I did not want them to become any drunker. They didn't like the idea, and tried to run a bluff on me, saying they would saddle up their horses and kill me, and run the d——d place themselves, if I would not give them anything more to drink. I told them I was running the place and would be there when they returned. Out they all went for their horses, and I prepared to give them a warm reception when they returned. It was in the summer and the weather was very warm.[4] My partner, Lock, was sleeping on a blanket on the ground just outside the rear of the saloon, where we had living apartments, and overheard all the crowd had said. I armed myself with a Winchester, two six-shooters, and a shotgun, then raised the window and awaited their coming. I could hear them riding along, and was prepared to cut loose at them as soon as they came in sight. Lock had not as yet said a word to me, but when the sound of the horse's hoofs rang out on the night air, he stepped in with his Winchester under his arm and asked, "How are you fixed?" I replied that I was fixed O.K., and he said he was ready for them. Knowing where I slept, they rode right up to the window, whereupon I jumped right out among them with two six-shooters, threatening to kill every one of them if they didn't drop their guns. They all complied when they saw I had the drop on them. There was a big, loud-mouthed fellow in the crowd, who was responsible for starting all the trouble, so we ordered him to leave town immediately. He accepted the order without a word and departed at once. Now that it was all over, the boys were feeling all right and insisted on staying. They unsaddled and it was two days before they left. During these two days I took in $200 and I had no more trouble. That was the last trouble I had with the cowboys while I was in the saloon business.

Business continued good, and I had no more fights in the saloon for some time. There were two rival merchants in the town, whose names were Clark and Martin, and both were regular patrons of the bar. Both were anxious to have me "boost" for them; but to "boost" for one was to lose the trade of the other, and I turned them both down. As they visited the bar frequently, they would often meet there, and invariably quarreled. One night they met in the saloon, and nothing would do but they must fight it out. I agreed to let them fight, if they would strip and go into the back room. And I further agreed to act as referee, and stand for fair play. When both were stripped, I called time, and they went at it. They were pummeling each other at a merry clip, when I opened the back door and pushed them both out. The yard was full of sand-burrs about an inch deep, and over they went, rolling in the sand-burrs. When they got up, they were a sight to see, all covered with sandburrs and madder than "wet hens." I shut the door in their faces and refused to give them their clothes. They were still full of fight, and concluded to go over to Clark's store and fight it out. A camp-meeting was being held just below the saloon, and as the fight occurred at the time when the people were coming home from the services, they were compelled to pass through the crowd to reach the store, where they had agreed to finish the fight which the sand-burrs had so unceremoniously caused them to temporarily abandon. They did not seem to mind the people, as they were mad, and determined to get down to business again without delay. The church people were completely flustrated at first, and the women blushed their deepest. Their escorts, however, enjoyed the situation immensely, and took to "joshing" the naked fighters for all there was in it. As it was evident that something had happened, the men hurried their wives home and returned to the saloon for particulars. They discussed the situation over their drinks until a late hour, and the bar did a thriving business. Next morning I took their clothes over to their respective stores. They both had black eyes, bloody noses, etc., and were pretty badly punished. The floor of Clark's store, where the melee was continued, was strewn with broken candy jars, candy, flour, etc., and presented as sorry a looking sight as the principals. They were separated before they could decide which was the best man, so I thought I would act as peace-maker and set them right before they got together again. I made them both come over to my saloon and shake hands over a social drink. They were reluctant to make up, but I insisted, and after we had several drinks they were to all appearances all right again. They were very sore on account of their experience with the sand-burrs, which stuck into their flesh like needles, and it was several days before they fully recovered from the effects. Martin was afterwards murdered for his money, while Clark got into two fights in succession and killed his man each time, then left the town, and was never heard of in that section again.

About this time Lock and I received an offer to sell out, which we accepted, clearing up a nice little sum of money. We then went to San Antonio and invested our money in sheep. We drove them to a point in Shackelford County, above Fort Griffin, and started in to raise sheep. We were allowing them to run over the range without protection, when we were surprised by a snow-storm. Snow fell to the depth of sixteen inches, and it was bitter cold.[5] When the weather cleared and we went out to round up our flock, we found that half of them had perished in the storm. We skinned the dead sheep, and by selling their pelts saved ourselves from a total loss. This experience with sheep was enough for us, and we sold out at the first opportunity. As the saloon business was pretty good, and not likely to freeze up, we determined to try it again, so we went to Mobeetie and opened up.[6] Mobeetie at this time had only three or four residences and a couple of stores, but there was one vacant building and we rented it. There was another saloon in the village, and that was owned by Henry Fleming, the sheriff.[7] We prospered in spite of competition, as whisky was still 25 cents per drink. and there were plenty of customers. I got tired of it after a time and sold out to my part-ner,[8] to accept a position as deputy sheriff under Fleming. In those days the rough element was in a majority and it took con-stant watching to keep them in order.[9] Every county did not have its sheriff and deputies as now, and Fleming had twelve attached counties to cover. His territory took in all the northwestern part of Texas to New Mexico and No Man's Land.[10]

My first experience as deputy sheriff worth recording took place soon after my appointment, when United States Marshal Johnson, of Dallas, and Deputy Marshal Courtright, of Fort Worth, together with two others whom they had deputized for the occasion, and a squad of soldiers under Lieut. Flipper, the only colored commissioned officer in the United States service, arrived in Mobeetie and began arresting merchants and cattlemen by the wholesale.[11] They were running low in the way of fees, and their plan was to arrest everyone they could on some trumped-up charge, and take them to Dallas, where they could be fined, and the marshal and his deputies would fatten off the fees. They had all the merchants and county officials in the country under arrest, except Tom Riley, a deputy sheriff, and myself.[12] The county was almost depopulated, and it was 150 miles to the nearest district judge, where a writ of *habeas corpus* could be secured. It was "up to us" to keep the marshal and his deputies from getting the men out of the county, and the marshal promised to take the prisoners to Fort El[l]iott, where he would hold them, to give us an opportunity to have them released on bond. We suspected, however, that he would do nothing of the kind, but intended to kidnap them; so we drew up a bogus writ of *habeas corpus* for use when the occasion required. That night about 12 o'clock they got their prisoners out of town and started to steal into the Indian Territory with them. They succeeded in getting out of town without being discovered; but when about three miles out, a druggist by the name of Rhinehart[13] escaped, and, riding back to town, awakened Tom Riley and me. I saddled my horse, and Riley took the horse Rhinehart was riding, and we started in pursuit. About a mile out of town we met Courtright coming back, and, recognizing his horse, he demanded it. At the same time we sprung the bogus *habeas corpus* and demanded his arrest; but, instead of submitting, he wheeled his horse and rode for his party. We were right after him, and as we neared the soldiers, Courtright yelled for them to shoot; but we were all running side by side and the soldiers could not tell which was friend or foe. In another second we were right among them, and they were so confused that they did not know what to do.

Taking advantage of our position, we lighted matches and read the *habeas corpus,* after which we arrested the whole bunch and took them back to town, where we turned the prisoners loose. The marshal and his deputies were "sore" over being knocked out of some nice prospective fees, and soon left town.[14] When the officers at the Fort at Mobeetie learned of the colored lieutenant's part in the affair, they immediately ordered him before a court-martial, which fired him from the service. He is now commanding a company in Old Mexico.[15]

The next party to come along and disturb the peace of Mobeetie was Wyatt Earp and "Mysterious Dave" Mathers, who had a lot of gold bricks they were anxious to sell to the good people in that vicinity.[16] Three of my friends wanted to invest in their bricks, but I advised against it, and removed the temptation by ordering the brick-dealers out of town. This move on my part came near causing serious trouble, as they were both desperate men, and had reputations all over the West. They finally left town, going down into the southern part of the State, where they were afterwards arrested while in the act of "roping in" some of Uncle Sam's good coin for a bogus brick.[17]

John Poe, now a banker at Roswell, New Mexico, and who was afterward associated with Pat Garrett in killing the notorious Mexican outlaw, "Billy the Kid," came to Mobeetie and was appointed deputy sheriff with me.[18] A few days later we started after a bunch of horse-thieves, and ran them up the South Canadian River and across the line into New Mexico. When they crossed the line, we gave up the chase, as we had no authority outside of Texas.[19] We returned to Mobeetie, and I took the stage for Fort Dodge, Kansas, where I could get a Santa Fe train for Las Vegas. We surmised that the horse-thieves would go straight to Las Vegas, as that was the only town in that part of New Mexico. It was my intention to go to Las Vegas and have them arrested, and recover the stolen horses. When I arrived there, I found that the fugitives had got mixed up in a little dance-hall frolic,[20] and had already been hanged, and their bodies buried. They were heavily armed, and, upon reaching the town, lost no time in starting something at the dance-hall. Joe Carson was city marshal then, and he started in to disarm them. He was shot nine times for his trouble, and turned and walked out into the alley behind the hall, where he fell dead.

During the melee the lights in the hall were shot out, but the proprietor, George Close, kept on firing at the bunch until he had two of them down, when the other two got to their horses and got away. The names they were known by were Henry, West, Dorsey, and Red. Henry was killed outright, and West was shot in the abdomen; Red and Dorsey made their escape.[21] They rode to an old adobe hut about nine miles from town, where they camped. Early the next morning a *posse*, led by Dave Ruderbaugh, [*sic*] started in pursuit and captured them in the old adobe hut. They refused to return to Las Vegas with the *posse* except with the assurances of protection, which were readily given by Ruderbaugh, and the party returned with the prisoners.[22] This little incident occurred in 1880, during the year of Grant's last campaign. President Grant had visited Las Vegas a couple of days before, and the officials had erected a platform in the center of town, from which he spoke.[23] This platform was still standing when the *posse* arrived with the prisoners, and they utilized it for a "necktie party." A long beam ran out from the platform and it was decorated with flags in honor of the distinguished visitor, and the horse-thieves were strung up side by side to this beam.[24] West, who had been wounded in the abdomen, was still alive, but in a dying condition. However, that did not make any difference, and they hanged him with the rest. As I had to go away around by Dodge City in order to reach Las Vegas, I arrived four days too late to witness the event, and they were all buried.

CHAPTER X

Life in New Mexico

As Las Vegas was without a marshal, the result of the dance-hall fracas, and in need of one badly, they offered me $12 per day, and I accepted the offer. The office of marshal in Las Vegas at this time was one of the worst to handle in the West, and even at the good salary they paid they had considerable trouble in keeping it filled. It was all a man's life was worth to make an arrest when a drunken row started, which accounted for the absence of the ever-present office-seekers.[1]

There were warm times in Las Vegas, as the Santa Fe Railroad was building through that country and had reached Las Vegas. The town was situate[d] about a mile from the point the railroad came through, and the Santa Fe was building a new town near the depot.[2] There were all kinds of people here and they were mostly a rough lot. I threw the town wide open and allowed all kinds of gambling. The streets were crowded with monte men, sluice games, shell men and fakirs of all kinds and descriptions. It was like an old Mexican town, only worse, and I permitted them to "whoop it up" so long as they submitted to being arrested and fined regularly for the support of the marshal and the justice of the peace. The fakirs and gamblers were so plentiful and prosperous that it was an exceedingly profitable job for me.

The justice of the peace was an old man named Steele, and he was as "right" as they make them.[3] Every time I made an arrest he would call me aside before the trial for information as to how much the prisoner had, and would fine him for the size of his "pile," only leaving him about two dollars for a fresh start. Our policy was to turn over one dollar to the county and divide the balance. We were doing a land-office business and having no trouble at all.[4]

One evening Pat Garrett, sheriff of Lincoln County, Jim East, and two other deputies brought in "Billy the Kid," the Lincoln County out!aw, together with Dave Ruderbaugh, Tom Pickett, Bill Wilson, and Tom Fowler, who were arrested for murder, cattle-stealing, and almost every other crime on the calendar.[5]

That night they placed them in jail in the old town, intending to take them to Santa Fe the next morning. Dave Ruderbaugh was wanted by the county officials at Las Vegas, as he, in company with a man by the name of Webb, had broken jail there a short time before and killed the jailer in making their escape.[6] It happened that I was the only native officer, all the rest being "Greasers." The next morning, when Sheriff Garrett went to get his prisoners to the train, the sheriff refused to let Ruderbaugh go, and, after a wordy war with Garrett, summoned half of the Mexicans in town to his assistance, in order to prevent Ruderbaugh's being taken away. Garrett, however, took Ruderbaugh along with the others, and reached the train without futher incident.[7] I went along to the train with the boys, as my sympathies were with Garrett, I having no use for the "Greasers." By this time the Mexicans were coming from all directions, armed to the teeth with every kind of a weapon they could find. I saw at a glance that there was likely to be trouble, so I went back to town and gathered up a few guns, with which I intended to arm the prisoners if it came to the worst. When I returned, they were crowded around the train and were loud in their demands for Ruderbaugh. I had my clothes and boots full of six-shooters, and, as they were not "on" to my game, I had no trouble in entering the car.[8] Pat Garrett then placed his gun against the glass door of the car and told them in his most forcible language that they could not have Ruderbaugh, and that the one who made a break to get him would make a good subject for a coroner's inquest. The train was standing on a side-track, and as it was a United States mail train, we had the United States marshal throw the switch and climb on the engine and open the valve. The engineer was one of the worst scared men I ever saw, and the outlook was certainly bad enough to frighten any peaceable man out of his wits. The United States marshal, not being used to running an engine, pulled the throttle half open the first jerk, and the train shot out on the main track at the rate of twenty-five miles an hour,[9] while "Billy the Kid" opened the window and let out a war-whoop that startled the

Mexicans, and they scattered in every direction.[10] When the train started, I jumped off and watched it out of sight. The sheriff and his Mexican crowd were a very much disappointed and disgruntled lot when they saw the train get away from them. They went back to town swearing in Spanish, but no one paid any attention to them.

As the prosecuting attorney was not "in" on the "divvy" of the gamblers and fakirs' fines, he did not like the idea of so much gambling in the town, and made an attempt to break it up. He hired a blockhead sort of a fellow to get the names of the gamblers, who was so clumsy in his work that all the boys soon "got on" to them. Between the old Mexican town and the new town the Santa Fe had built there was a thicket of willows, through which it was necessary to pass in going from one town to the other.

One night a well-known sporting man, who has since died, laid for the district attorney's "piker," and when he passed through the willows almost shot him in two. When searched, the dead "piker" had about 150 names in his pocket, as he had not yet made his report to his employer. That was the end of any attempt to stop gambling in Las Vegas, and even to this day the gamblers have not been bothered. As a result, Las Vegas is one of the best wide-open gambling towns in the country.[11] After two years' experience as marshal of Las Vegas, I got tired of the job and threw it up. Arthur Gilson [sic] was appointed in my place, and he proved to be a very good man.[12]

I next formed a partnership with George Close, the man who ran the dance-hall where Joe Carson, my predecessor in the office of marshal, was killed. We went to Socorro, New Mexico, where we opened a saloon and a gambling-house.[13] In Socorro there was a vigilance committee which was very vigilant. Besides hanging a man every day,[14] they came around every evening and collected $2 for each table before they would allow the games to open. As we were running six tables, we paid the vigilance committee $12 a day for the privilege of doing business.[15] This was a pretty high license, but the play was good, and there was not a night while we were in Socorro that we quit losers. I had an old Mexican, by the name of Juan Garsiere, dealing monte at one of the tables, whom the committee did not like, and one day, when Close and I were over to Albuquerque attending the fair, the vigilance committee came around and got him and hung him.[16] We were very "sore" when we found out what the vigilance committee had done, as we were paying them $12 a day for running the game, and did not propose to be molested in that way. We took our revenge in "shooting up" the town, running every member of the vigilance committee off the streets. We meant business too, and if we had found any stray members around the corners, we certainly would have fixed them.[17] The only thing they could have had against our Mexican monte-dealer was that a few days before he had assisted us in releasing a man from their corral whom they were going to hang. They had simply picked the man up on suspicion, because he wore long hair and a red handkerchief around his neck. According to their code, that was sufficient excuse for hanging a man, and when the Mexican told us about it, we immediately went to the corral and released him. From that time on the vigilance committee looked daggers at the Mexican every time they saw him.

A new camp was being started about forty-five miles southwest of Socorro, which was called Lake Valley.[18] We sold out our Socorro house and went down there. I was appointed marshal of the new town before there was a house built,[19] as the townsite was covered with tents only when we arrived. There were a number of rich silver mines at Lake Valley, and the town had all the indications of amounting to something, as well as keeping the marshal and the undertaker busy. The enterprising citizens soon started their buildings, and it was not long before quite a number of stores and residences were erected. My first duty as marshal was chasing two Mexican horse-thieves, who had stolen two horses and two mules from some prospectors who had stopped to enjoy the hospitality of Lake Valley for a few hours before proceeding on their search for the precious metals. I took the trail, and came in sight of them as they were nearing Alopas, a small Mexican town. When I got within shooting distance, I opened fire on them, when they leaped from their horses and took to their heels. I headed off the horses and turned them back toward Lake Valley. In doing so I had to jump my horse across an *acequia,* which is the Mexican name for an irrigating-ditch, and he slipped and fell with me under him. My foot was caught in the stirrup, and I lay half covered with water for an hour before I could get my foot loose. If the Mexicans had known of my condition, they would have made short work of me, as I was perfectly helpless. By twisting my horses's neck and holding his head in a certain position, I finally worked my foot out of the stirrup. After releasing myself, I rounded up the stolen horses and brought them to Lake Valley, where the prospectors were overjoyed to recover them. They bought a few rounds of drinks as a solace for the fall I had received, and we had a good time for the rest of the afternoon.

Lake Valley was built in a gulch, with high mountains on each side. One day, as I was riding down the gulch at the lower end of the town, I came across Tom Wilson[20] lying on the rocks, and so sick with pneumonia that he could not get up. He had both feet frozen off in the early days on the State Plains[21] of Texas, and was entirely helpless. I rode back to town, where I procured a buggy, and came back and got him. I had to find a warm place for him; and as the building boom had not yet set in, there was but one house in the town; that was a store building, occupied by some Chinamen. I took him to the Chinamen's quarters, and they would not allow me to bring him in, so I kicked them out. The Chinamen jabbered awhile and cursed me in Chinese until their vocabulary was exhausted, when they moved off up town to tell their troubles to someone else. I fixed Wilson up as comfortable as possible, and he recovered in a short time. The Chinamen didn't bother us further, as they were glad to be allowed to stay in camp, and we never saw them again until Tom was well, when we gave up the house. I saw Tom not long ago, and he thanked me for caring for him during his illness at Lake Valley, and we had a long talk over old times.

When the Chinamen got into trouble, I was the first man they hunted up, and afterwards they would do anything for me. One night some of the boys went to the Chinamen's stone mansion, and held them up for a bag of silver. As soon as it was over, the Chinamen came for me. They called me "Mr. Mackey," and wanted me to come to their house and protect them from any further hold-ups. I went along and stayed all night with them. They had $1,500 which the hold-ups failed to locate, and they were very much afraid someone would get it. We stayed up all night, and the Chinamen entertained me to the best of their ability. The next morning I advised them to take their money and leave it in the postoffice safe, for safe-keeping, as there were no banks there. To show their appreciation of my protection, they loaded me down with presents of all sorts of Chinese articles. The boys didn't like it very well, because I had offered protection to the Chinese, and there was considerable grumbling over it.

Major Fountain, an American who had married a Mexican, organized a company of militia among the "Greasers," similar to the Texas Rangers, but they did more harm than good.[22] They were an ordinary, murderous lot of "Greasers," and did not care whether a man was guilty or not, so long as they got an opportunity to shoot or hang him. One day they came over to camp and arrested three men on the charge of stealing ore and cattle. They were Butch Hill, John Watts, and old John Shannon, who had lived in Lake Valley ever since the town started, and were respectable citizens as far as respectability went then. They took them out of town and shot them to pieces, after which they stripped the bodies of clothing and cut them open, filling the cavities with tobacco spit; then placed quids of tobacco between their teeth. They left them lying in the middle of the road, with a placard on each one stating that any one who moved them would be treated likewise.[23] This was too much for me, and, as I wasn't afraid of Fountain or his bloodthirsty band, I got two miners, named Jack Shedden[24] and Fred Henry, to accompany me, and we went out to where the bodies lay and brought them back to town. After dressing them up nicely, we gave them decent burial. The town people were too badly scared to attend the funeral, and the only man who would have anything to do with it was a merchant named White. Lyon A. Sheldon was the territorial governor,[25] and when he heard of what we had done, he telegraphed Fountain to "kill McIntire on sight." The operator at Nutt Station, which was the nearest railroad point, received the message, and gave me the "tip." I avoided them for two weeks, during which time I went to Albuquerque, where I met General John A. Logan, who had come down to that country to look over the Western Slope of New Mexico, which an Eastern syndicate he was connected with had recently purchased.[26] Logan offered me $10 per day to go with him on a scouting trip over the slope. Jim Courtright, one of the deputy marshals who attempted to arrest all the men in Mobeetie, Texas, when I was a deputy sheriff at that point, was also hired in a similar capacity.[27] We rode over the Slope with General Logan for two weeks. There were three cattle-thieves on the Slope, one Indian and two white men, and I received a "tip" on them from one of the settlers, and arrested them. I then left General Logan to take my prisoners back to Albuquerque, where I landed them in jail.[28] While in jail, they made an affidavit stating that Jim Courtright and I killed some Mexicans while scouting with Logan, and that gave the Territory Militia another chance at me.[29] I knew that it would not do for them to get hold of me, so when General Logan returned to Washington, I returned to Lake Valley to attend to some business, and Courtright accompanied me.

I resigned the position of marshal, and Courtright and I decided to take a trip up to Kingston, which was a new mining camp twenty-eight miles farther up in the mountains. Before starting, I was appointed a U. S. deputy marshal,[30] and was given some papers to serve in Kingston. My wife[31] accompanied us on the trip, which was made by stage. After we were there two days, I sent Courtright back to Lake Valley on business, and on his arrival he was arrested by Major Fountain's Mexican Militia. They didn't want him very bad, as I was the one they had orders from the governor to kill on sight. I was to have taken the stage the next day to return to Lake Valley, when a friend, knowing the Mexicans would waylay the stage, rode up to Kingston and told me about it. Instead of taking the stage next day, my friend and I, mounted on fast horses, quietly rode into Lake Valley that night. It was very late when we reached the town, but my friend managed to communicate with Jim in regard to getting him out the next night. The Mexicans were allowing him considerable liberty, and we had no trouble in making our arrangements. I remained in hiding the balance of the night and all the next day, with two good horses and everything ready to rescue Jim at the first opportunity during the night. The friend who rode to Kingston and notified me of what the Mexicans did saved my life, as the next day they rode out about six miles from town, where they awaited the arrival of the stage. The spot they chose was in the vicinity of some nice, large trees, any one of which would have done for a "necktie party." My wife came down on the stage, and when they reached the point where the Mexicans were in hiding, the "Greasers" rushed out and surrounded the coach. As they did not see me, they searched under the seats, on top, and every place a man could possibly hide. They were very much chagrined to find that I was not in the stage, and, after questioning the driver, allowed him to drive on.

When it became dark, I had a friend to notify Jim to be at the back door of a certain saloon, and in readiness for my coming. The Mexicans were watching him all the time, but were a short distance away. I was leading Jim's horse and rode quietly to the vicinity of the saloon without the Mexicans seeing me, when I made a dash up to the door, where Jim was standing waiting for me. He "hit the saddle" without waiting for me to stop, and we were off like lightning.[32]

The Mexicans were taken by surprise, and before they could recover, we were firing our six-shooters right and left. They were completely "bluffed" and ran in every direction, hiding in any old place to get out of sight. We made for the top of a convenient mountain, where, with the aid of a large, powerful field-glass, we watched every movement in the valley. During the night we would quietly steal into the town and get what provisions we needed. We stayed on the mountain top for three days, watching the movements of the Mexican Militia. The company numbered seventy-five Mexicans, in command of Major Fountain and Lieut. Patton[33] who were American. They knew we were still on the mountain top, but they realized the strength of our position, and were afraid to attempt to take us. The second day they left, and came back on the third reinforced to the number of two hundred. That number was too strong for us, no matter what our position might be, for two men could not possibly fight two hundred. It meant death for us to fall into their hands, so we pulled out for Old Mexico, heading for the "Bad Lands," where our trail would be lost in the soft sand. We traveled all that night and until 3 o'clock the next afternoon without water for ourselves or horses. The weather was extremely hot, and our suffering was intense when we reached a railroad water-tank on the line between El Paso and Deming, New Mexico, where we found an old prospector, who was on his way to Lake Valley. He had five burros and a lot of canteens, and as the water-tank was built high up, and no way of getting water out of it quickly, we refreshed ourselves from his canteens. I then climbed up to the tank and found a big nail, which I pulled out and let a small stream fall to the ground. When we watered our horses, and the old prospector filled his canteens, I climbed back and put the nail back, plugging the hole. Next morning I tried to buy one of his canteens, but he refused to sell one at any price. He seemed to be very grouchy about the matter, as he had plenty and was going into town, where he could get all he wanted, while we were just on the edge of the "Bad Lands," which we could not hope to cross without water. As he would not sell, I did the next best thing, and threw my six-shooter down on him, taking the best canteen he had. We took his guns and bade him a courteous "good-morning," also telling him that we would leave his gun about three hundred yards away, so he couldn't do anything in the way of recovering the lost canteen. We traveled all day across the "Bad Lands" under the broiling sun. Our horses were again suffering for water, and there was no relief in sight, only a great sandy desert on all sides as far as the eye could see. About dark we saw a section-house in the distance, and headed for it. It was surely an oasis where we could refresh ourselves with water and food. We rode up, and politely asked if we could have something to eat for ourselves and water for our horses. The section foreman who inhabited the place replied that he had nothing to eat, and very little water, as the railway company furnished him water in barrels and the supply was getting low and would barely last until his next consignment would arrive. I told him there was nothing to it; that we must have some food and water; and he directed us to a Chinese hut, a little farther down the track, saying we might find something there. He was working all Chinese on the section, and when we arrived they were in the midst of an exciting game of fan-tan. The doors and windows of the "Chinks' " residence were all on slides, and they were as well protected from hold-ups as possible. They had been held up so often, a Chinaman always being considered legitimate prey in this country, that they were badly scared every time a stranger happened along. We rode right up to the windows, which were so high that we could just see in, and watched their game of fan-tan, without our presence being discovered. I stuck my head through the open window and yelled, "Hello, John!" They were so surprised that they couldn't say anything but "Who! Who!" like a bunch of hogs; and, thinking they were being held up, all made a rush to close the windows and door. Jim had backed his horse away a few paces, and called to me: "Come away, Mac, or you will get shot!" But I was determined to get some water and food, if there was any to be had; so I rode around to the door, and hammered and knocked for some time, without getting any reply. At last, becoming impatient, I shot up in the air, and told them that I was an officer of the law, and only wanted a drink of water. A rather weak voice answered from within the hut: "You no hurtee me, me lettee you in." I assured them that I would not harm them, and they opened the door. I assumed the air of an officer, and inquired if they had seen any horse-thieves in the vicinity. Of course they hadn't, but the fact that they thought I was an officer pleased them. They had plenty of water, and we filled our canteens and watered our horses. We then "braced" them for something to eat, and they gave us some pickled pork, which seemed to contain more salt than pork, and a pan of bread which was merely flour and water baked as hard as a rock. We only rode a short distance from the Chinese quarters to camp for the night, as it was so dark we could not see where we were going. After staking the horses to the saddles, we made an attempt to eat the bread, but a file wouldn't touch it. We couldn't break it with our hands, so we laid it on our bootheels, taking our six-shooters and breaking it in pieces. We then took the pieces and soaked them in water until they were soft enough to eat. The bread and pickled pork did not make a very delicious repast, but we were hungry enough to eat anything. When we left the Chinese quarters, we headed straight away from the railroad, but in the intense darkness had wandered off our course. Early the next morning a passenger train came along and we awoke to find that we had camped about twenty feet from the railroad track. We lost no time in jumping into our saddles and crossing the line into Old Mexico. We did not travel far until we saw a lot of Mexican soldiers, all in white uniforms, coming straight toward us. We put the spurs to our horses and got away. The border on the Mexican side was patroled by guards, and a constant watch was maintained to prevent anyone from coming or going without passing through the hands of the customs officials. We had just gotten out of sight of the soldiers when we ran into a customs river guard. He ordered us to halt, in Spanish. Our answer was to pull our six-shooters and order him to go around us, which he did without a murmur. We were then in the hills, approaching El Paso del Norte,[34] which we soon reached. There we gave our horses a good feed and plenty of water. While they were resting we strolled out into the town and filled up on *mescal.* After "punishing" all the vile Mexican "booze" we cared for, we saddled up and started for El Paso, Texas, just across the river. We had to pass the custom-house to get across the river, but as we didn't care to pay any duty on our horses, guns, etc., we failed to stop. The officers on duty at the custom-house, seeing us ride by, rushed out and ordered us to halt; but I answered in Spanish that we were only going to the river, about two hundred yards away, to water our horses, and would come right back. We kept right on going, while they stood and watched us. When we reached the water, we still kept on going. They then saw that they had been tricked, and rushed into the building to get their guns to take a shot at us; but by the time they got back we were on the Texas side with our guns drawn, and they didn't dare to shoot.

It was about noon when we found ourselves safely on the Texas side, so we rode a short distance away from town, where we camped until dark; then went on into El Paso. After putting our horses in a livery stable, we took a walk down town. In making the rounds, we met a lot of Texas Rangers, all old friends. They treated us fine, and if their friendship was measured by the number of drinks they bought, it was all anyone could ask; and they proved that it was. Governor Sheldon, of New Mexico, wanted us so badly that he had offered a reward of $1,000 for us, dead or alive.[35] Just before leaving Lake Valley, I had exposed the governor and his Militia through the little paper published there, and now the papers all over that part of the country had copied the article, giving it widespread publicity. [36] This had angered the governor more than the burying of the men his Militia had murdered, and he was determined to get us at all hazards. El Paso was a dangerous ground for us with a price of $1,000 on each of our heads, but the Rangers, being our friends, would not think of attempting to arrest us or "give us away." While we were with them, we were as safe as we could be anywhere. We were anxious to get home, however, and sold our horses and took the train for Colorado City, Texas. As we had to keep under cover, we had the Rangers arrange with the conductor to let us occupy the little smoking-room at one end of the coach and allow no one else to enter it. We paid $15 for the use of the room during the trip, and as the conductor was also our friend, we were not molested. We stayed at Colorado City two days and called on some friends. From there we went to Fort Worth, where we stopped with a friend.[37] I had previously notified my wife to meet me in Fort Worth at the home of my friend, who was an officer, and she was there when we arrived. When it became known that we were in Fort Worth, the excitement ran high, but the people were our friends, and we were not molested. After staying with our friend a short time, we took up our residence in a thicket just back of the graveyard until the excitement died down, as we were liable to be surprised and captured at any time. We remained in the thicket during the day, and slept in the graveyard at night, with a grave for a pillow. Mrs. McIntire, together with my friend's wife, would bring us provisions, and we were completely lost to the people of Fort Worth. Two nights, when we were making a lodging-house out of the cemetery, it rained, and we slept in a vault.

The excitement began to gradually die away and in a short time we were not thought of. Jim made application for a position on the police force and was appointed, and I left for Wichita Falls, Texas, where I opened a gambling-house. Luck was with me and I won considerable money during my short stay here. One day I got a tip that they were after me, and I left between two days, going to Shreveport, Louisiana. My wife met me here, and we went down to New Orleans. From New Orleans we took passage on the *William Kiled* for Cincinnati.[38] The river was very high, and the second night out, as we were at the supper-table, the boat struck a snag in trying to make a landing, and went down. The water was up, almost overflowing the banks; the night was dark as pitch, and the wind was very high. The pilot ran her nose into the bank at the right place, but before the deck-hands could tie up, the wind blew her around until she hit the snag, which was under water, and could not be seen. As we were all at the supper-table when the accident happened, the dishes and food were scattered all over the floor by the force of the shock. The excitement was indescribable for a few seconds, and everyone rushed out to see what had happened. The boat's carpenter hurried down into the hold to ascertain the damage, and soon called out to the captain that a hole nine feet long by four feet wide had been stove in her bottom. With this information, we made preparations for leaving the boat, as it was a foregone conclusion that she would go down. Luckily, we were close to shore, and all got off safely, and in a few minutes she toppled over, leaving about half the deck out of water.[39] The only shelter in sight was a big cane-brake, where we stayed four days before we were picked up.

The only habitation near was that of an old colored woman. She had about one hundred chickens, which we bought. After these were eaten, we subsisted on red haws, paw-paws[40] and pecans. There were twenty passengers, including four women, and the officers and crew. A "Diamond Joe" boat[41] passed up the river and we signaled it to stop, but as there was considerable bad feeling between the "Diamond Joe" and other lines, the "Diamond Joe" officers refused to pay any attention to us. On the fourth day we were all half starved, when a boat belonging to the same line as the *William Kiled* came along and took us on board. When we reached Cincinnati, we took another boat up the Ohio to Pittsburg[h]. After short trips up the Alleghany [*sic*] and Monongahela rivers, we visited points in West Virginia, Ohio, and Kentucky, including my old home in Brown County. After visiting relatives and friends for nearly a year, we returned to Texas.[42]

CHAPTER XI

Captured by the Rangers

On my return to Texas, I located in Wichita Falls, where I "ran a game" in the White Elephant saloon.[1] Everything went well, and I was making money, until one day, when I was in a little side-room of the saloon carving a turkey for the free lunch, the Rangers rushed in from three doors and covered me with their guns.[2] They allowed me time to straighten up my business, then took me to their camp just below the town. I was popular in Wichita Falls, and my arrest was the talk of the town. Nearly everyone in the town came to the saloon as soon as they heard the news, and many accompanied me down to the camp. The next day they took me to Fort Worth, and twenty-five of my friends went along. When we arrived at the Fort, we learned that they had caught Jim Courtright in much the same manner as they took me at Wichita Falls. They enticed him into a room to look at a picture, and while he was admiring it, they put their guns to his head and arrested him. The town of Fort Worth was in an uproar over the arrest, and didn't like it any better than the people of Wichita Falls.[3]

The city and county officers were all our friends, and they planned an escape for us. The whole town was on the streets, and nothing else was talked of. The police had planned for Jim and me to eat supper together, but my train was late, so they held Jim's supper back as long as they could without exciting suspicion. Finally, when they could not hold back any longer, they took Jim in to supper, and, as he was playing for time, that was the slowest meal he ever ate. Five Rangers and four city officials were eating with him, and the Rangers were watching him closely. The city officers, who were "in on the deal," had placed two six-shooters under the table for Jim,[4] and I had provided two fine horses for the escape, a black and a gray, which were standing outside.[5] Jim delayed the supper all he could, and ate and ate until he came near bursting, and still I did not come. Finally the Rangers grew impatient, and insisted on starting for the depot. When Jim saw he was "up against it," and couldn't wait for me, he accidentally dropped his napkin, and stooping down to pick it up, he came up with two six-shooters, covering the Rangers. He had the "drop" on them and backed out, keeping them covered. He mounted the gray horse and made good his escape. He wasn't heard of around Fort Worth for two years.

The Rangers were all raving mad, and came to the depot to await the arrival of the train upon which I was coming. They swore by all that was good and holy that I wouldn't get away. When my train pulled in to the depot, there was the biggest crowd there to meet me that had ever filled that depot. Every hack was filled with officials, and I was lionized by everyone except the Rangers. The city officials did the proper thing, and secured a writ of *habeas corpus,* which prevented the Rangers from moving me for eighteen days. On the way from the depot to the jail, the Rangers covered me with drawn revolvers all the way. An immense crowd followed us, and in a few minutes the whole town had gathered around the jail.[6] The Rangers were afraid the mob would break down the jail doors and release me, so as soon as the crowd dispersed, I was moved to the new jail at Decatur. This jail was considered the strongest that could be built, and there was a reward of $1,000 for the man who could break a bar. After I had been in the Decatur jail a few days, eight bars were broken, but it was discovered, and no one appeared to claim the reward. There were thirteen other prisoners in the jail, and the five Rangers, two deputies, and the jailer were guarding us.

About 12 o'clock the first night after the bars were so mysteriously broken, the Rangers and deputies were all sound asleep in the hallway. There was a big iron door between them and the cell-room, which they kept open, so they could see the prisoners from where they slept. They slept with their guns by their sides, and did not even dream of any attempt being made to escape. The jailer wore a long mustache and a large beard.[7] He was armed with two six-shooters. The bars were broken in the corridor behind the bath-tub, and I had to invent an excuse to get to the bath-tub. Everything was quiet, and everyone fast asleep but myself

and cell-mate and the jailer. The time was ripe, and I had my
cell-mate play the sick act. He worked up an awful fever in a few
minutes, and I called the jailer, telling him of my mate's alleged
condition, and asked for permission to go and get him some water. He let me out into the corridor, and I got a bucket and went
to the bath-tub. Instead of drawing water, I pulled the bath-tub
away and started to crawl through the hole made by the broken
bars. I was in my underclothes, and had a big silk scarf with a
knot in it and a towel, with which I intended to gag the jailer,
stuffed into my drawers, so I would have my hands free. I got
stuck in the hole, and it took some hard tugging to release myself.
In the meantime, my cell-mate called the jailer and asked him for
some whisky, in order to attract his attention from me. I was
stuck for only a few seconds, but it seemed like an hour. When I
got loose, I took a different tack, and put one arm and shoulder
through first and then squeezed the rest of my body through. Just
as I got out, the jailer, thinking I was an unusually long time in
getting water for a man who was suffering with fever, came down
the corridor looking for me. He was holding his lamp in front of
him, and it must have blinded him, for he called, "Where is
Mac?" without seeing me. I was now outside the iron part of the
jail. I thought the jailer had seen me and would arouse the Rangers, so I ran around the cage and grabbed him by the mustache
with one hand and choked him with the other. I choked him so
hard he could only grunt, then picked him up and carried him
around behind the cage, where I threw him down and gagged him
with the silk scarf. I put the knot into his mouth, then tied the
scarf around his head. On top of the handkerchief I tied the towel,
gagging him so completely that he could not utter a sound. I then
took his suspenders off, and with them bound him to the cage. I
threw his guns down where I first caught him, and, after picking
them up, went back to where the Rangers were. They were still
sleeping soundly, and my first thought was to take their guns
away from them. I was afraid of waking them, so I pulled the
door shut gently and secured the keys from the top of a cell,

where the jailer kept them when not in use. I unlocked the cell doors and released every prisoner in the jail except one, a horse-thief, serving out a five-years sentence, who had "peached" on a scheme I had planned to get out the night before. After getting the men out of the cells, the next thing in order was to dig through a two-foot stone wall with a case-knife. I started in on it, working like a beaver. It took fully an hour to make an opening in this wall, but I thought it took a week. While digging on the wall, I had the boys bring the jailer around and tie him to the cage, where we could watch him. They brought him all right, but instead of tying him to the cage, they tied him to a water-pipe that was only nailed to the wall with small nails. When we had a hole large enough for a man to crawl through, we all stripped and threw our clothes out, then crawled through and dropped to the ground, fifteen feet below. We were then in the jail-yard, which was surrounded by a board fence about twenty feet high. It was smooth on the inside, with nothing to cling to, so scaling it was out of the question. We ran around to the front of the jail, putting on our clothes as we ran, where there was a gate by which we could get out. By the time we reached the gate, the jailer had broken loose and awakened the Rangers. They jumped up and started for the jail door, but I fired a shot from a six-shooter, which struck the door uncomfortably close and they drew back and closed the door. I was the first to pass out of the gate, and was just passing through when I fired at the jail door. As my shot had somewhat disconcerted the Rangers, the moment's delay gave us all time to get out, and we were soon lost in the darkness. The Rangers were soon out and shooting right and left, but as the night was very dark and cloudy, they could not see us, and no one was hit. My cell-mate, whose name was Henry Tickle, and I separated from the rest, and "pulled out" for Fort Worth.

We had not gone far when we discovered that they had put bloodhounds on our trail. We were not afraid of bloodhounds, as I was armed with two six-shooters, one of which I turned over to my partner. We were both large men and left footprints much larger than the rest, who were all small men, which enabled our pursuers to discover the fact that they were on our trail. However, they didn't want any of our game, as they knew we were armed, and called their dogs off, to keep them from being shot. After giving up our trail, they turned their attention to the rest of the boys, and, with the aid of the dogs, captured all of them. It was the night of July 12, 1884,[8] and two days later we reached Fort Worth, where a friend, who is now one of the most popular and best lawyers in that city, hid us in the opera-house. Tickle remained in the opera-house two days and then left, going south. About six months later, I learned that he had been literally shot to pieces, in an attempt to capture him, by local officers in southern Texas.

I stayed in the theater ten days, and passed my evenings in watching the play from a peep-hole. After hiding ten days, I grew bolder, and stopped with friends around town. One night I slept in the next room to the captain of the Rangers. He was hunting me, and I overheard him talking to others about me in the next room. I only traveled about at night, and was always disguised. One night, as I was stepping off a street car, the Ranger captain and his lieutenant got on. They looked at me sharply, but did not penetrate my disguise, and I passed on. I stayed in Fort Worth about a month longer, and saw and talked with the police every day of that time, but, as I was only wanted in New Mexico, they did not offer to arrest me.[9]

From Fort Worth I went to Denison, where I played the games at the White Elephant saloon.[10] The officers of Denison were all right, and I stayed there for two months. Special officers, hungry for a little piece of money, came after me several times, but I always got the "tip," and evaded them There was too much money offered for my capture to allow me to stay in one place long at a time, and finally it got too warm in Denison, and I had to get out. A "spotter" arrived in town one night, and I got the "tip," and, as it was only a question of days when I would have to move anyway, I resolved not to take any more chances; so I hired a horse and rode to the second station out of Denison on the Texas Pacific Railroad. There I bought a ticket for Shreveport, Louisiana, and took the first train. From Shreveport I went to Baton Rouge by boat, and from there took a Mississippi River boat down to New Orleans.

CHAPTER XII

Again in the Toils

At New Orleans, I stopped at the City Hotel, where I met a friend whom I knew in New Mexico. This friend, not thinking of getting me into trouble, told a friend of his who I was, also that there was $10,000 reward offered for me, and cautioned him not to "give me away" to anyone. His friend could not keep a secret, however, and told another party, and in another day it was the common topic of the town. My friend was mistaken about the amount of the reward, as it was only $1,000, instead of $10,000, but the officers, thinking it was $10,000, were all the more eager for my capture. The officers were not the only ones looking for me, and it seemed as if the whole town was on my trail. I determined to get out of town as soon as possible. The weather was extremely hot, and I took off my guns and changed clothes, putting in a light linen suit. I then went down to a steamship ticket office and bought a ticket to the Honduras River.[1] The ship was to sail at 3 o'clock that afternoon, so I walked slowly back to the hotel, packed my clothes, and prepared to leave after dinner. I was on the lookout for a surprise, and watched everything around the hotel, but nothing looked suspicious, so I ate my dinner without thinking of the dangerous position I was in. On finishing my dinner, I rose from the table and went to the toilet-rooms. While there, five big, stout men pounced upon me unawares; they grabbed me in all sorts of positions and twisted my arms and neck around, until I thought they would break. When they were sure they had me, they picked me up bodily, and, without buttoning my clothes, carried me through the dining-room out to the street, where a carriage was in waiting. My appearance in the dining-hall with pants hanging down and person exposed created consternation among the lady guests at dinner, and they screamed and ran pell-mell for their rooms, knocking over tables and breaking dishes as they went.

I never will forget the noise of the breaking dishes or the excitement which followed my forced trip through the dining-room in my unpresentable condition. The officers who caught me didn't care for modesty or anything else, so long as they had captured Jim McIntire. They were a badly scared lot, and held on to me like grim death, even after we got into the hack. They didn't give me a chance to button up until I was safely locked up in the police station. They were still very much excited and didn't know what to do with me, but finally decided to put me in the parish prison for safe-keeping, until they were sure whether I was the man wanted or not.[2] Anyone who has ever been in New Orleans knows what the old parish prison is, but for the benefit of the readers, who haven't been there, I will say that it is the worst in all this broad land. It was run according to the old French rules, and its regulations were severe. It was damp and unhealthy, and when a man was incarcerated there, it was a question whether he ever came out alive or not. Often a man would be arrested for a trivial offense, and thrown into the parish prison, where he would be held for nine months without a hearing, and during this time no one would be allowed to communicate with him. While incarcerated there, I witnessed some of the most cruel and barbarous scenes of my life. There were two men in the prison, named Ford and Murphy, who were to be hanged in a few days, and they tried in every way possible to get a respite.[3] In their desperation, as the time drew near, they circulated a report that I had secured a lot of dynamite, and had planned to blow up the jail and release the prisoners.[4] The prison officials, on hearing this report, took out all the prisoners thought to be implicated in the plot and "stocked" them, in an attempt to make them confess and reveal the details of the alleged plot. The stocks were made of two heavy blocks of wood, with notches cut out large enough to hold a man's legs. The two blocks were on hinges, and opened and shut like a clamp, leaving two holes about two feet apart, in which a prisoner's legs were placed. They tied the prisoners' hands behind their backs and, compelling them to lie down, fastened their legs in stocks at a point about six inches above the ankles, which left that much of the legs and feet protruding. They would then tie a rope around one ankle, and, loop it around the other, would give the signal to a big negro, whose weight was about 250 pounds, to pull on the rope. Then would come the most excruciating agony I ever witnessed. With a steady pull, the negro would by degrees use his whole weight on the rope, gradually bending the bones until the feet almost touched. This cruel practice would cause the prisoners to shriek and scream with pain. Their sufferings were horrible to behold, and I hope I shall never be forced to see it again. They had three pairs of stocks, but only "stocked" two prisoners at a time.

In the meantime, they searched me carefully every day, as well as every nook and corner of my cell. One day, as they were in the act of searching me, I took a turn at "joshing" them, as they had never seen dynamite, and had only a vague idea of what it was like. They didn't like to be "joshed," and for revenge put me in the stocks. I just laughed at them, and dared them to put the rope on me, as I was a New Mexico prisoner, and they might have gotten into serious trouble had they done it. When I "bluffed" them out of putting the rope on me, they decided to put me in a cell by myself on the next floor above.[5]

The sufferings of the boys in the stocks touched me deeply, as they could not walk even at the time I left and were crippled for life, all on account of a lie two murderers had circulated.

On the twelfth day of my incarceration in the parish prison, "black sheep" Sheriff Davis, of Wichita Falls,[6] came to New Orleans to attend the carnival. The officers got hold of him and brought him to the jail for a look at me, and he identified me at once and told them all about me.

When I was positively identified, they communicated with Governor Sheldon, of New Mexico, and he issued requisition papers, which the governor of Louisiana promptly recognized. Then they were worried as to how to get me back to New Mexico without taking me through Texas. They were afraid to pass through Fort Worth, as my friends there would, in all probability, "lay" for us and provide a way for my escape. They finally decided on a route by way of St. Louis, and we passed through five States before reaching Santa Fe. I was in irons all the time during the trip, and when we arrived in Santa Fe, I was at once taken before the governor, still manacled. Gov. Sheldon was awaiting our arrival, and greeted me with a broad sarcastic smile, saying, "That is the man I want," He appeared to be very happy over my arrest, and paid the $1,000 reward right there. He gave them Territory scrip, which they cashed at a discount of $200, leaving $800 to divide between them. They then took me to Albuquerque, where they delivered me up to the jailers, and returned home.[7]

My Albuquerque friends wanted to get me out, and the vigilance committee wanted to hang me. Both parties threatened to make trouble, and the sheriff,[8] in order to prevent either one from getting me, placed a strong guard around the jail, with orders to kill me if any attempt was made on the jail.

That made it look bad for me, and as I did not care to take chances of being shot down like a steer in a pen, I shoved a $50 bill into the jailer's hand, and he gave me two 45-caliber six-shooters and a box of cartridges. With these I felt easy, as the jail was an old adobe building, with walls about four feet thick, and the door was merely an opening just large enough for one man to pass through by stooping. With my two six-shooters I could have kept this hole full of dead men, if an attempt had been made to storm the jail.[9] I was left at the jail Saturday night, and my bond fixed at $100,000. The following Monday my friends had the bond reduced to $5,000. It took less than an hour to secure bond, which was signed by Mayor Geo. A. Laile and others, who were strangers to me.[10] It happened that none of my friends were real property owners, and as the bond had to be signed by owners of real estate before it would be accepted by the court, the mayor and his party came to my rescue and signed the bond. I staid around Albuquerque until the next term of court, when I was discharged, as the State [territory] could not make a case against me. I had done nothing but bury the murdered men at Lake Valley in defiance of the Governor's orders, and the court could not see wherein that constituted a crime.[11]

CHAPTER XIII

In a Shooting Scrape

After the trial I left Albuquerque, going to El Paso del Norte, Mexico, where I dealt a faro bank. I only stayed here a short time, and then went to Mobeetie, in the Texas Panhandle, Texas. In Mobeetie I bought two fine race-horses and put them on the track. I won forty-two races without losing one; consequently my pockets were bulging out with money. One day Jim Wilkinson and I took a run over to Harrold, Texas,[1] where I got into a shooting scrape with Johnny Davidson and his brother-in-law, whose name I have forgotten. We were "shooting craps," and the bets on "come seven, come eleven" were heavy. The bones were rolling right for us, when Davidson's brother-in-law, who was a heavy loser, became very abusive. He singled out my friend as the object of his abuse, and, as he would not stop, I knocked him down. That "stirred up his animals," and was the beginning of a "hot time." Davidson and his brother-in-law rushed out for their guns, saying they would be right back. While they were gone, my friend and I sauntered up to the bar and I ordered a drink of whisky. Just as I started to raise my glass, I looked in the mirror behind the bar, and saw a Winchester rifle sticking in the door just behind me. I dropped my glass and jumped sideways, then ran for the door, where Davidson shoved his rifle up against my stomach and fired. I was too quick for him, however, and ducked my stomach back and he missed me. It was dark and I could only see his arms, one of which I broke with a shot from my six-shooter. He then ran back into the darkness, but kept on firing. I could only locate him by the flash of his gun, while I was in the light and ought to have made a first-class target. I exchanged shots with him for a few minutes, when I broke the other arm and shot a nipple away. This was too much for Johnny, and he turned and ran for another saloon. I followed him, but when I reached the saloon all the fight had been taken out of him, and he asked me not to shoot. I replied that I wouldn't, and thought it was all over. They were not through, as I found out later; for the first thing they did after I left the saloon was to telegraph to

Vernon,[2] Davidson's home, which was about fifteen miles up the road, stating that I had killed Johnny Davidson. A number of Davidson's friends immediately started for Harrold, with the intention of avenging his alleged death.

I was waiting for them when they "hit the town" and mixed right in with them, giving them no chance to do anything. I stayed right with them, going from place to place, and never let them get the "drop" on me. As we were drinking freely, we finally all got drunk and "passed up" our troubles. They were as friendly now as they had been hostile before, and some of their crowd got so full that I had to throw them into their wagons when they started home. The next day after our return from Harrold I took my horses and rode up to Tascosa,[3] on the South Canadian River, to run a race. While there, I was arrested for shooting Davidson. I promptly gave bond, and remained in Tascosa until court convened at Vernon, which was the county seat. I went down to Vernon with the judge, several attorneys, and officers. We traveled overland, across the State plains,[4] in buggies, wagons, and horseback. We had to pass through a rough stretch of country, which was inhabited by all kinds of wild animals, before we struck the plains of the South Canadian. Just as we were approaching the "L. X."[5] ford, where the road was washed out, making a bank about four feet high on one side, while the other was a wall of high, rocky bluffs, our horses began to snort and to exhibit signs of fear. We were looking ahead to see what was alarming the horses, when a large Mexican lion ran across the road, and crouched by the side of the bluff. The beast licked his chops and angrily waved his tail, as if inviting us to come on and have it out. I rode around and slipped up behind him, while the rest of the party held his attention. I got within ten feet of him before firing, and felt sure I could break his neck with a shot from my six-shooter. I shot him square in the back of the neck, but the ball, instead of penetrating his neck, glanced around and came out in front, and it only bewildered him. He then ran up on the bank on the other side of the road, and crouched down on the edge

of the bank. One of the deputy sheriffs joined me, and we crept
up the side of the bank until we were within leaping distance for
him. All the time he lay watching every move we made, but did
not attempt to get away or charge us. When we were as close as
we dared to get, we both opened fire at once. He leaped for us;
but, while he was in the air, we sent three or four well-directed
shots into him before he lit. He fell right between us, but was so
badly wounded that he could only strike at us with his paws. He
died in a few seconds. He was a fine specimen, measuring 9 feet
8½ inches in length.

The rest of the journey was made without incident or adventure, and when my case was called in court on the charge of
shooting Davidson, it was dismissed; but the judge fined me $35
for "rolling the bones" ("shooting craps").[6]

From Vernon I went to Panhandle City,[7] up on the State [*sic*]
plains, where I opened a gambling house and raced my horses. I
made all kinds of money here, which I invested in cattle and
horses, and had accumulated some good-sized herds. One day
John Jones, an old cow-puncher friend of mine, came along. He
was Texas born and bred, and free with his money both at the bar
and gambling-table. He enjoyed a touch of frontier "high life"
now and then, and we drank together, ran pony races, and enjoyed ourselves in more ways than one. Jones was such a good
fellow that no one ever quarreled with him, and everything we
did was for the fun there was in it. It made no difference who
won in the pony races or at the gaming-table, the same good
feeling prevailed. Jones picked up a "sucker" from the East one
day and brought him in where I was dealing monte. The "tenderfoot" belonged in one of the large Eastern cities, and thought he
was one of the wise ones. I had a large amount of money stacked
up on the table, and the seductive game of monte looked easy to
him. He "sized me up" for a native, and together with Jones,
started in to pick up some "easy" money. I had no limit, and met
all bets that were placed. I was dealing myself, and did not feel
uneasy over the outcome. When the Eastern man concluded he

had had enough, I was $700, an overcoat, and a watch "to the good." I divided up with Jones, and we managed to take a little trip over to Amarillo.[8] The Eastern man was very "sore" over his loss, and the more he brooded over it the more certain he was that he had been "skinned." He told Jones he believed the dealer had robbed him, and Jones replied, saying, "I know he did, d——n him!" Mr. Eastern Man then made a proposition that he and Jones kill me, when we alighted from the train at Washburn, where we had to change cars.[9] Jones agreed and helped him lay the plans. We were all to take the same train, and when Jones got an opportunity, he "put me next" to the details of the plot.

Washburn was merely a junction, and the depot consisted of two box-cars, with a prairie for a platform. There wasn't a settlement for miles, and the only inhabitants in the vicinity, besides a small hotel and saloon, were cowboys who didn't know the word "farmer." They were only looking for unbranded cattle, monte games, whisky, tobacco, dance-halls, and pony races. The Easterner asked Jones if he was armed, and he replied that he was not; as the Easterner had a six-shooter and a pair of brass knuckles, he offered Jones his choice, and Jones took the knuckles. When we arrived at Washburn, it was very dark, and Jones and his man left the train first. When I stepped off, they were waiting for me, and Jones had got around behind the fellow, ready to hit him if he made a move to shoot. I knocked the man down before he could pull his gun. He scrambled to his feet and disappeared in the darkness, and we never heard from him again. We took the next train for Amarillo, where I sat in a poker game and made a big winning. When the game broke up, there was "nothing doing" in Amarillo, so we took the first train for home. At Washburn, while we were waiting between trains, we walked over to the hotel to pass away the time, and met George Berry, an old friend who was "mine host" at the Junction Resort.[10] Mr. Berry is now an alderman of the upper house in Kansas City, Missouri. We had a few drinks together, and then a few more, till we got pretty well "jagged." When dinner was announced, we went to the dining-room. Berry's help were all sick, with the exception of a Chinese cook and a small innocent looking girl, who couldn't have been more than twelve or thirteen years old, waiting on the tables. As we were pretty well "hooked up," the soup tasted pretty good to us. We ordered a second bowl, and when the girl went for it, the Chinese cook got up on his dignity and threw a soup-bone at her. I resented this sort of treatment, and proceeding to the kitchen, grabbed the Chinaman by the queue. I wrapped the queue around my hands and led him out in the yard behind the hotel, where I was going to behead him with my pen-knife, when Berry appeared on the scene and talked me out of it. I still held him by the queue, however, and led him around into the saloon, undecided whether to kill him or not. After another drink of whisky, I decided not to kill him, and led him out on the porch, where I cut his queue off and then kicked him off the porch. The "Chink" was almost scared to death, and considered himself lucky to get away so easily. He took to his heels and never showed up in Washburn again. We drank at the bar until train time, when Jones and I returned to Panha[n]dle City.

Panhandle City was a lively burg about this time, and there was always something going on. We had dances, horse-racing, and trap-shooting at glass balls and clay pigeons. We held regular tournaments and offered prizes of $50, $30, $20, and $10, respectively, for the four best scores. I always managed to pull down the $50, as I was an expert at the traps. One day, after the shooting was over, I matched my pony, "The Deuce of Hearts," for $100 in a two-hundred-yard race. My partner, known as "Smoky Jim," [11] who was to ride him, was so drunk that he could hardly sit up in a buggy, but, as the pony was very fast and would run almost as well without a rider as with one, I wasn't afraid to take the chances. There was a large crowd present, and, as the race was between my pony and Henry Adde's, a cow-puncher, who also had a good horse, the betting was lively. I made a flash bet that "Smoky" would fall off the pony, and one of the crowd took me up. "Smoky" overheard the bet and thought it was "on the square." The ponies were off a minute later, and "Smoky" wanted to win the bet, so he let go his hold on the reins and started to fall; when he saw he was going to be hurt, he tried to regain his hold, but it was too late, and he hit the ground, rolling over and over. The pony kept right on running, and won the race. A number of us ran out to where "Smoky Jim" was lying, stunned by the fall, and brought him into a saloon. He was badly bruised and the skin was broken in many places. We brought him to his senses with whisky both inside and out, and after working over him for awhile, he was able to walk with assistance. That fall knocked all the racing out of him, and he never rode again.

The Santa Fe had just completed the Southern Kansas branch through the western part of what is now Oklahoma Territory, and the country was thrown open for settlement. I left Panhandle City for Woodward, Oklahoma, at the time of the opening, and was one of the first settlers to arrive.[12] There was nothing to Woodward but a depot, but it grew into a town right from the start.[13] I opened a saloon and cold storage house and secured the agency for a popular Milwaukee beer. I wholesaled and retailed whisky, beer, and ice, and did a thriving business. One day I received a good offer to sell out, and, as I wanted to take a trip to Hot Springs,[14] I promptly accepted the offer.

At Hot Springs I lived high and "blew in" my money, playing the races and almost living over a gambling-table. I lost considerable money and after awhile grew tired of the place. From Hot Springs I went to Mountain View, Oklahoma Territory,[15] where I opened a gambling house that did a thriving business, as all territorial gambling-houses did. Mountain View was the center of the small-pox district, which disease was epidemic at that time. There were over 300 cases of small-pox in the vicinity, but the disease was in a mild form and no deaths resulted.

CHAPTER XIV

Through Heaven and Hell

The ordinary small-pox was a common disease among the Indians, and no one there paid any attention to it. I had been in Mountain View just twelve days when one of the boys was stricken down with black small-pox. I was also seized with the dreadful disease, and before its spread could be checked, there were thirty-five of us in the pest-house, which consisted of a mere "shack" and some tents just outside the town. The black small-pox was considered sure death, and the appearance of the disease created widespread consternation in Mountain View. Everyone who could get away left the town on short notice, and those who remained were in constant fear of contagion.[1]

The territorial board of health provided us with nurses who had formerly had the ordinary small-pox, but there was nothing else that could be done, as there is no treatment known to medical science that will cure the disease. The nurses cared for us as best they could and allowed the disease to run its course. Five days later one of the boys died, and in twelve days they were all dead except myself. I lingered for thirty days, my flesh slowly rotting and dropping off the bones, until I was a horrible sight to look upon. The flesh on my fingers, heels, and toes all dropped off, leaving the bones exposed, and my entire body was a raw mass of sores. Chunks of my flesh had rotted off in many places and my once stalwart form was now little more than a skeleton. I did not suffer any pain, but was very weak. On the thirtieth day my heart ceased to beat and I lost consciousness. I was pronounced dead, but I did not know it, and arrangements began for my burial.

My life had been one of adventures and thrilling scenes, but it was my fate to now behold the unseen world in all its resplendent glory on one hand, and all its indescribable hideousness and terror on the other. The soul of man does live—though it be not in the body—and there is a hereafter, where it goes after death in this world.

When I died, I felt a hand on each of my shoulders, which

picked me up and took me flying through space. I offered no resistance to the unseen hands, and experienced no fear in my flight, though it seemed that I was moving a hundred times faster than anything moved on earth. Finally I could see a great light of peculiar brilliance in the distance, which I surmised to be Heaven. The effect was beautiful and filled me with wonder. I was traveling straight toward it, but when I was still a long way off, I felt my speed suddenly slacking, and in a short time I alighted on the ground before two large fiery pits; each one of which seemed about one hundred and fifty yards long, fifty yards wide, and fifty feet deep, with stone walk six feet wide between them and surrounding them on each side. The bottoms of the pits were covered with fire, which blazed up ten or fifteen feet high, and resembled burning oil. There were a number of planks fastened together, which led up to this walk from the ground a few feet below, and on each side of the chute two dragon-like angels of the Devil were stationed. There were people coming almost all the time. They marched up in squads and singly, while these hideous monsters, reaching out and catching them in their long claws, would throw them into the fire. The women were thrown into one pit and the men into the other. An unseen hand took hold of me and ushered me out on the arch between the two pits, three or four steps from the end. When we stopped, I asked who it was with me, and the answer came in a hoarse, discordant, but plain voice. "The Devil; be not afraid." Just then I was seen by one of those dragon-like reptiles, and it came after me, but the voice ordered it back. There were five of them in each pit, and they were the most hideous-looking things I ever saw. They were all different in color, and their heads were shaped differently. All were of the same size, except one, who seemed to be the leader of the pit. They were about thirty feet long, and would weigh about a ton, while the leader, a big gray one, was twice as large. They resembled a dragon in shape and appearance, and their heads and fore-quarters were large. They had large mouths with long teeth, and great claws on each foot. They stayed in the fire, except when they saw anyone they would rise up just like a fish in water, without any exertion, and grab the unfortunates, throwing them into the fire. As I walked along this walk they came after me several times, but the voice ordered them back; then they would dive into the fire, stirring it up so it would boil and blaze higher. The pit I was looking into was filled with men, and every time one would venture toward the edge, hoping to escape, a blow from one of their long tails would knock him back into the fire. It puzzled me to know what became of all the people who were thrown in, and they were all in a row up and down the center of the pit. The number in the fire did not increase, no matter how fast the new arrivals came in, and I began to look around for dead bodies, but I could not find any.

It was an awful spectacle to look upon. Men were groaning with pain and their contortions were pitiful. I could look down into their faces and see the terrible look of agony each one expressed. The fire did not consume their bodies; it only tortured. It was not hot where I was, though I was standing on the walk between the two pits, which were only six feet apart. I noticed there were no children in the pit with the men, so I turned around and looked into the women's pit. There were no children in the women's pit, and neither were there any dead bodies. The scene here was more heart-rending, if possible, than the men's pit, and I stopped a minute to watch them burn. The women were scrambling and climbing over each other, all the time piercing the air with their screams and shrieks for help. Oh, the suffering I witnessed there! Words cannot be made to adequately picture the scene. No earthly torture could begin to compare with it, and the thought that these poor souls would spend eternity there sickened me. The fire boiled up every few seconds, and the flames shot up just the same as they had on the men's pit. Either the draft or the force of the flames was so strong that the women could not keep their hair down, and it stood straight up, waving back and forth in the flames; but it was not even singed. I walked on toward the other end of the pits, watching the seething, boiling mass of flames as I walked, and wondering how people could live and suffer in that fire without being burned. I kept looking to see if I could discover any dead bodies of little children; but when I got far enough along to see every part of both pits, I made up my mind that there were no children in Hell, and that life there was everlasting torture. It relieved my mind greatly to know that there were no children suffering the punishment of that terrible place, and I reasoned that if there were none there already, none would go in the future. Parents, whose children, so dear to their hearts, have departed from this world, need have no fear as to the future for these dear ones, as eternity for them will not be spent in a hell of fire. I saw with my own eyes, and know that I am not mistaken.

A few feet from the end of the pits I stopped and looked back, and the big gray guard of the pit saw me for the first time and came after me. He opened his mouth and rolled his eyes at me, as if he was sure of his prey. He looked far worse than all the rest, and when he rose up close to me, I felt that my time had come; but the hands again touched me on the shoulders, and I felt myself rising in the air as if by the wind. Hell soon disappeared from view, and I was glad that I had escaped its horror. The course I was traveling seemed a little to the left from the direction I had first taken, and though no words were spoken, I could feel the hands on my shoulders, and knew some one was with me. After traveling for some time, I found myself on the ground in front of immense double stone gates. These were the gates of Heaven, and I stood for a few seconds admiring them. The gates were set in a massive stone wall, which was so perfect that it could only be Nature's work. It did not resemble a stone wall on earth, and it was solid, without cracks or mortar seams.

As I was looking at this wonderful piece of masonry a loud, clear voice sounded right near me, although I could see no one, and asked, "Who are you?" "My name is James McIntire," I replied. "What do you want?" said the voice. "I am very thirsty," was my reply; and then I asked, "Who is it I am talking to?" The

answer came back in a soft, melodious voice, "This is God."
"God, where are you?" I asked, as the voice seemed right by my
side. God did not answer my question, but asked where I was
from. I answered, saying: "God, I have died on earth from the
black small-pox and was then taken to Hell. After being shown
that place, I was brought here." The voice then asked, "What
did you do on earth?" "I have done almost everything imagin-
able, both good and bad," I replied. "I have been accused of
almost every offense on earth, but I have been good to everybody,
refusing nothing I had. I have been selling whisky and gambling
of late—" Here He interrupted me, saying, "There is no harm in
either of them." I then asked what day of the week it was, and
God replied that He knew nothing of such things. "God, the only
Bible that You have given us teaches that there are certain days
of the week, Monday, Tuesday, Wednesday, Thursday, Friday,
Saturday, and Sunday, which is the Sabbath, and a day of rest,"
said I. He again replied that there was no such thing. I next told
him that we had thirty days in a month, and twelve months in a
year. "There is no such," He said; "there is only light and dark,
and when tired from toil, rest." The only question I asked Him
which He did not answer was, How long do those people who are
in Hell have to be tortured in that awful fire?" I waited for some
time, hoping God would answer; but as He did not, and thinking
He had not heard, I asked the question over again. All remained
still, however, and I thought He had gone. As I was thirsty, I
spoke again, saying I was very thirsty. Almost immediately the
immense gate swung open and I was again directed by the unseen
hands, which I could feel on my shoulders. I was ushered through
the gates of Heaven, and there my eyes rested upon a scene of
beauty, happiness, love, and peace, which will never grow dim
in my memory. "It is beyond the power of words to describe such
beauty and no artist could portray it as I saw it. The grandeur of
the scene, the richness of the colors, and the rare beauty of the
flowers and trees, etc., made me feel happier than I ever had been
on earth. Goodness and content permeated the air and there was

joy and gladness on every hand. No one could see Heaven and ever doubt the existence of God, the Supreme Being who rules the universe. It made an impression on me which will be with me always, and I know I shall see it again.

There were two beautiful walks, one of gold, and one of stone, leading from the gate to the finest fountain I ever saw, about five-hundred yards from the gate. The golden walk was as straight as a straight-edge, while the stone walk made a slight detour and met the golden walk at the fountain. There was a slight incline from the gates, which I ascended, and from there I had a full view. The grounds were laid out like a park, but no landscape-gardener on earth could secure such a beautiful effect. Between the two walks, which were about ten feet apart, was a row of large rose-bushes all in full bloom. The roses were larger and prettier than I ever saw on earth, and were all of different colors. Such radiant floral beauty could not exist anywhere except in Heaven. On all sides were orange-trees, beautiful shrubs, plants and flowers of the prettiest varieties.

On the golden walk, beside the beautiful roses, hundreds of angel babies were playing, laughing, chattering, hugging and kissing each other, and all together expressing a degree of happiness I had never witnessed before. They were all clothed alike, having wings of a cloud-gray color. They were like so many happy birds, and when I approached, would chatter and fly away, lighting a little further down the golden walk. I was interested in the little ones, and the fact that I found them all in Heaven, while there were none in Hell, touched the tenderest chord in my heart. I kept on trying to get close to them, and they finally arose and flew over me to a long row of orange-trees, a short distance to the right of the stone walk, where they alighted in the tops of the trees. The trees were loaded with large luscious-looking oranges, and presented a most beautiful appearance with all these baby angels perched on their branches. As soon as they settled down, they all began singing and playing. After allowing my eyes to feast on the scene for a few moments, I felt thirsty again, and as

I saw an orange fall occasionally, I thought I would walk over under the trees and pick up one to quench my thirst. When I stepped on the grass, I noticed that it was not only a more beautiful green in color, but softer and more like velvet than any grass on earth. The lawn was also so much smoother than any earthly lawn, and was absolutely perfect. Not a wilted blade of grass or an uneven spot ever so small could I find. I was walking very slowly, intensely interested in everything I saw, when, looking up, the air was filled with millions of people robed in that beautiful cloud-gray, the same as the little ones, and with wings of the same color. I stopped and watched them. Some were flying around leisurely, while others were in groups, standing still, and apparently engaged in conversation. One never got in another's way, and so graceful were their movements that, no matter how many were in the air, they could fly around with ease and never clash. There were men and women of all sizes, the same as they had been on earth, and all were clustered around a central figure. There were many baby angels mingled with the larger ones, and they were the picture of happiness. They were flying around, laughing, talking, and lighting on the larger angels' backs. The central figure was that of a man about thirty feet in height, with larger wings in proportion. He was robed the same as the others, and floated slowly through the air, while all the others hovered around him.

I was looking at the true and living God in His heavenly home, and was so pleased that I could hardly take my eyes from the scene. My thirst again reminded me that I must relieve it, and I walked on towards the orange-trees where the baby angels were sweetly singing, still watching the scene above me. When I neared the trees, I turned my attention to the little ones, thinking to get up close and speak to them; but when I would get within a certain limit, they would all rise and fly away to trees. I walked up to the trees they had just left, and the ground was covered with the finest and largest oranges I ever saw. I was so thirsty I couldn't resist the temptation, so I reached down and picked one up. I was holding it in my hand, about to peel it, when I looked up, and God and His angels were slowly descending. As they were coming directly towards me, I momentarily forgot my thirst in watching their movements. They were settling down all around me, and I stood still, holding the orange, until they should come close enough for me to speak to them. In another second they were quite close, and I called to them; but they seemed to be enjoying themselves so much and so intensely in one another that they paid no attention to me. I wanted a drink of water, and, as I could not make the angels listen to me, I thought I would eat the orange to quench my thirst. I started to press my thumb into it to burst it open, when the orange disappeared. I was surprised, and stooped down to pick up another; but just as I touched it, they all disappeared.

I looked up, and the angels were floating around over my head as low as the tree-tops. I could see them very plainly and distinguish their features, just the same as I could a lot of people around me on earth. The babes did not pay any attention to me, but were continually prattling and fluttering over the older ones' backs. The grown-up angels, however, looked at me pleasantly, as if they knew me, and some of their faces seemed familiar. There was a gulf between us, however, and I could not talk with them. The air was completely filled with them as far as I could see. Some were old and some young.

Finally I could stand it no longer, and said in a loud voice, "I am thirsty." The words had barely passed my lips when I felt the unseen hands once more grasp my shoulders, and I was marched over to the stone walk, and on to the fountain. All the angels followed me to the fountain and hovered over it by the millions. The fountain was built of solid stone. I estimated it to be seventy-five feet high and fifty feet in diameter. About every four feet around the fountain there were holes where the water poured out into the basin, and at each one of these there was a golden cup attached to a silver chain, which was fastened to the stone walls of the fountain.

When I took up one of these cups to drink, the angels all around began a chant which was the sweetest music I ever heard. I could not understand the words, but their sweet, melodious voices harmonized so perfectly, and the air was so entrancing, that I enjoyed it as I never enjoyed music before. What could be more fascinating than angels singing heavenly music amid such beautiful surroundings? One did not have to be a music-lover to appreciate such singing.

I drank copiously of the water in the fountain, and it, like everything else I had seen in Heaven, was so much superior to the best water on earth that I couldn't compare it. I can only say that it was so sparkling and refreshing, so good and pure, that I could hardly get enough of it. After drinking three large cupsful, I set the cup down, when the singing ceased and a voice asked if I had drunk enough. I replied, that I had plenty. The voice must have come from the one whose hands rested on my shoulders, as it spoke right into my ear, though I could not see anyone except the angels, who filled the air.[2] I was then ushered back along the stone walk over which I came. The golden walk was again filled with the little children, playing as I had first seen them when I entered Heaven, and it seemed to be their play-ground exclusively. As I started back the angels who were floating about in the air struck up another chant and followed me, all the while chanting even sweeter than before. They hovered close around me, many not over thirty feet from the walk.

I walked slowly down the stone walk toward the gates, the hands still resting on my shoulders and guiding my footsteps. When I reached the top of the incline leading down to the gates fifty feet farther, the music ceased. I was stopped and another pair of hands were placed on my head, pressing very hard for an instant, then dropping to my shoulders. I can shut my eyes and feel the sensation of the hands pressing my head just as plain even to-day as I did there in the beautiful Heaven, so great was the impression it made upon me. Another voice, presumably the one which belonged to the hands now resting on my shoulders, then asked: "Do you want to stay here or go back to earth?" I was confused and did not know what to say, as I did not want to leave such a beautiful place, such joy and happiness, and such ease and comfort, to return to a world where everything is work, worry, and strife. While I hesitated something told me to go back to earth, and I replied: "I would like to return to the world I came from." The voice then told me to be good on earth and I would come back again. The angels again chanted sweetly, and I turned and took another look at the innocent angel babes playing glee-fully along the golden walk by the roses. Suddenly I felt myself lifted up by the hands on my shoulders, and we went over the stone wall, flying through space. The return trip to earth was all in darkness, and I knew nothing until I awoke and found Dr. Abur-nett,[3] one of Oklahoma's leading physicians, working over me.

Although I was practically dead for but ten minutes, my spirit seemed to travel for hours. I surprised the doctor by coming back to life, and even then he did not expect me to live. For a long time my life hung by a thread, and the doctor had no hope of my recovery; but Providence had ordered that I come back to earth and live to relate what I saw, and I eventually recovered. After thirty days, I was strong enough to be moved, and could walk a few steps at a time, with the aid of a cane and a crutch. At this writing, more than a year later, I have not fully recovered my strength, but am enjoying good health, and weigh almost as much as I did prior to my sickness.

Conclusion

In concluding the story of my life, I deem it proper to make a statement for the benefit of the readers of this volume. I have told this story as completely as my memory served me, and given the details just as they happened.

The first thing I want to impress firmly on your mind is that there is a hereafter. Those who are privileged to visit the unseen world and return again are few; and I must have been chosen for this vision on account of my wickedness, as I believe I was the hardest-hearted sinner on earth. I have done everything that was good, also everything that was bad. On one side, I have been charitable to everybody, and never saw anyone suffer if I could help them. I have often discommoded myself to help others, and would share my last crust; while on the other hand, I have stolen and robbed;[1] I was sold for murder in New Mexico, and brought a good price, but was exonerated.[2] I have killed Kiowa and Comanche Indians by the score, and skinned them to make quirts (whips) out of their hides; and I once killed and skinned a squaw and made a purse of her breast, which I carried for nine years. I slept in a cemetery, using a grave for a pillow, and when it rained I slept in the vaults; that was when I was a wolf and the hounds were hunting me. I have had a very busy life from boyhood, and there are few men who have gone through what I have.

Now, I must believe what God told me in regard to the days of the week, not censuring the Bible as a book, for there are many good things in it; but from what I saw and heard, it is not all true, and there are many passages which are merely man's individual opinion, purporting to be the words of God. The Bible says: "God created all people alike." If that is true, why did He treat the first settlers of our land differently? The Indians were the happiest people on earth, and, just as God said, they knew nothing of the days of the week, nor the Bible; they knew only daylight and dark, the sun, moon, and stars. Although the Bible performs a mission on this earth, I cannot believe all there is in it, after seeing for myself, and conversing with God. It keeps people

civilized and in harmony, but again, it is the most vulgar piece
of literature we have on earth; it is an obscene book—so obscene
that the laws of the United States will not permit its being carried
through the mails. The postal authorities will not allow the Bible
to be mailed if they can help it; but, as I said before, there is
much good in it, and it serves a good purpose on earth.

Before I was privileged to view Heaven and Hell, I was as
thorough a non-believer in the existence of a God as Ingersoll.[3]
All the sledge-hammers in the world could not have beaten into
my head the fact that there is a life after death. I was taken and
shown both places, and I am now convinced. I also want every
reader of these words, who has lost little ones by death, to know,
when you lay down at night and think of them, that they are safe
and happy in Heaven. I saw myriads of them in Heaven, of all
sizes and ages, and all enjoying happier hours than they ever did
on earth. There are no children in Hell.

God told me at the gates of Heaven, that there was no harm
in drinking or gambling, and I expect to enjoy those sports as
long as I live. There is no harm in anything, unless you make
harm out of it. I believe that God knows how I am talking to you,
and feel that He sent my spirit back to this earth on this mission.
My heart feels light and I am happy to place this volume before
you, because it is a positive truth.

To those who were living under the same belief that I was
prior to my revelation, I want to state that you are mistaken; once
more I say, there is a Heaven and a Hell, and I hope my state-
ments are convincing enough to make an impression on your
minds and cause you to change your belief.

The minister of the gospel picks out a few texts and preaches
from them. He says he is preaching the Bible, but he only
preaches what suits him; in most cases he dare not tell his con-
gregation the truth or he would be out of a job. They wear a pious
look, and attempt to make people believe they are good all the
way through, but besides not preaching the truth as they find it,
they often drink and carouse the same as the wickedest of men. I

have smuggled many a preacher a bottle of whisky or a case of beer, but I don't cheat in that way. As a class, when they are away from home, they are the biggest lot of hypocrites of any class of people on earth. It is a common thing for a preacher in a strange town to wink at you and ask "on the quiet": "Where can I find a trusty hack-driver?" and in the same breath, with another wink, tell you: "You know, I want to be sure and be awakened before daylight, as I am traveling on a pass and don't want to get left." I hate to tell on such innocent preachers, but I have had such incidents happen so often that I believe it is my duty to expose some of the hypocrisy. They will tell you that the church is a holy place, but when the devil's breath in the form of a cyclone sweeps across the prairies, it wipes out the churches, but never touches a saloon. If I saw a cyclone coming up, I would run for a saloon rather than a church. They preach that Sunday is the seventh day of the week and a day of rest, but all calendars and science teach that Sunday is the first day of the week. Then different races and religions have different days of the week which they call Sunday. The inconsistency of such teaching is apparent to every one who will calmly give the matter a few minutes' thought. All denominations construe the Bible differently, and none of them believe alike, although they claim to be preaching from the same book. What liars or fools they must think the others are! However, it is all in the game; and just like the politicians—they are out of the money.

My conscience tells me, and my experience proves it, that to be a man, be fair and honorable with your neighbor and true to yourself, and you will be a Christian. Christianity as practiced by the ministers wavers, but the man who invariably follows the dictation of his conscience has the true religion.

I consider one school-teacher worth a hundred preachers. I have heard the expression that preachers are not worth their salt, but that is comparing them with too good and useful a commodity, even if it is cheap. Salt was used in all offerings, and is not only incorrupting in itself, but it prevents corruption. It is an emblem of purity, fidelity, and stability, for it preserves instead of destroying; it gives itself away for the good of all that is associated with it, the same as Christ redeemed the world, and is, therefore, not to be compared with the class of hypocrites known as preachers.

Notes

Editor's Introduction

1. "The McIntire Publishing Company" was established solely to produce this book. Hoye's Kansas City Directories for 1901–1903 list no publisher by that name. Today, copies of *Early Days in Texas* are very rare, and none has appeared for sale in years. The book has therefore been absent from dealer price guides, but if a copy in good or better condition were offered for sale today, it would probably have a value of $500 to $700 (Richard Morrison, Austin, Texas, book dealer, to Robert K. DeArment [cited hereafter as RKD], April 6, 1990).

2. Texas historian T. C. Richardson wrote in 1943: "I am inclined to believe McIntire's narrative to be accurate as could be expected as to facts, but he is woefully lax as to dates" (T. C. Richardson to Mrs. J. M. Porter, October 16, 1943, quoted in Millie Jones Porter, *Memory Cups of the Panhandle Pioneers*, 70).

3. Charles A. Siringo, *Riata and Spurs*, 189.

4. Eugene Cunningham, *Triggernometry*, 208.

5. J. Marvin Hunter and Noah H. Rose, *The Album of Gunfighters*, 158.

6. *Albuquerque Journal*, June 8, 1885.

7. Siringo, *Riata and Spurs*, 189.

8. Charles A. Siringo to E. P. Lamborn, April 4, 1923 (Lamborn Collection, Kansas State Historical Society, Topeka, Kansas).

9. Siringo, *Riata and Spurs*, 189.

10. Ramon F. Adams, *Burs Under the Saddle: A Second Look at Books and Histories of the West*, 472.

11. F. Stanley to P. J. Rasch, October 18, 1963, quoted in Philip J. Rasch, "Murder in American Valley," *English Westerners' Brand Book* (April 1965): 6; F. Stanley, *The Lake Valley (New Mexico) Story*, 8.

12. Msgr. Stanley Crocchiola to RKD, March 20, 1990.

Author's Preface

1. Loving, Denny, Berry, and Poe are mentioned later in the book, and background information on them is provided in notes at the appropriate places. The reference to "Mr. Reed, an intimate friend at Mobeetie, Texas" is apparently to W. H. Weed, who was an early arrival at Mobeetie (or Sweetwater, as the town in the shadow of Fort Elliott was known at the time), where he opened a saloon (Ida Ellen Rath, *The Rath Trail*, 165). Weed later built a general merchandise store which he operated in conjunction with a retail and wholesale liquor business; apparently on Sundays he did a little preaching. "Rev. W. H.

Weed of Sweetwater, Texas, is in the city and has purchased lumber for a new business house," said the *Dodge City Times* of October 15, 1878. "The liquor business is good, he reports. . . ." By 1881 the *Times* was referring to Weed as "the big merchant of Mobeetie" (October 6, 1881), enjoying "a big business in the Pan Handle" (January 29, 1881). "He intends establishing a store at White Oaks, and look on the mountains when they are high," the paper said on March 17, 1881, and reported later in the year that, in a move "of great importance," he had sold his business: "Mr. Weed's stock was immense, composed of general merchandise, amounting to \$35,000" (December 1, 1881). Weed did relocate to White Oaks, New Mexico, where he opened a large general store (Morris B. Parker, *White Oaks: Life in a New Mexico Gold Camp, 1880–1900*, 45).

2. Writing in 1901, McIntire was actually forty-seven; he was born in 1854.

3. On the title page the author's name is given as "Jim McIntire" and the publisher as the "McIntire Publishing Company," with the surname spelled with an "i"; nowhere else in the book is the name spelled with a "y." This is undoubtedly a printer's error. Although many contemporary legal documents and newspapers as well as secondary sources spell the name "McIntyre," the signature on Texas Ranger payment records is consistently spelled "McIntire."

Chapter 1. My Start in Life

1. In the very first sentence of his narrative McIntire misinforms. He was born in 1854, eight years later than he states. His parents, James W. McIntire, aged twenty-one, and Grace McColgin, twenty-nine, were married in Brown County on November 16, 1848. Grace (or Gracy as she was known) gave birth to three sons: William, in 1852, Isaac, in 1854, and John, in 1856. The second son, Isaac, would reject his given name and adopt the name of his father, James (Patricia R. Donaldson, *Brown County, Ohio, Marriage Records, 1818–1850;* U.S. Bureau of the Census, Seventh Census [1850], Population Schedules, Brown County, Ohio; U.S. Bureau of the Census, Eighth Census [1860], Brown County, Ohio).

Why "Jim" McIntire would choose to misrepresent his age by eight years is anyone's guess. Perhaps figures confused him; throughout his book he is consistently inaccurate when citing dates and distances, but he is much better with names.

Brown County is one of the counties in the extreme southern part of Ohio, lying on the Ohio River about forty miles east of Cincinnati.

2. On September 6, 1863, Gracy McIntire died at the age of forty-four, when Isaac (Jim McIntire) was only nine years old (Lillian Colletta and Leslie

Puckett, *Tombstone Inscriptions of Brown County, Ohio,* 273). James W. McIntire, who had originally married a woman almost a decade his elder, now took a much younger wife, Sarah, fourteen years younger than himself. The move to Ironton, where McIntire became a grocer, occurred in 1868 (U.S. Bureau of the Census, Ninth Census [1870], Population Schedules, Lawrence County, Ohio).

Ironton, on the Ohio River seventy or eighty miles to the east and upriver of Brown County, is the county seat of Lawrence County.

3. John White, several months younger than "Jim" McIntire, was the son of Stephen White, a brick mason of Ironton, and his wife Ellen. The Whites had raised a family of seven children, of whom John was the next to youngest (Eighth Census [1870], Lawrence County, Ohio).

4. McIntire means West Virginia, as he states correctly later. West Virginia achieved statehood in 1863, and this minstrel show tour by McIntire and Johnny White took place about 1870.

5. Catlettsburg, county seat of Boyd County, Kentucky, is located ten or fifteen miles southeast of Ironton, at the confluence of the Big Sandy River and the Ohio, very near the corner where the states of Ohio, Kentucky and West Virginia meet.

6. J. C. Eastham was sheriff of Boyd County in 1870 (Janet Ingles to RKD, January 3, 1990).

7. Gen. John H. Morgan of the Confederacy set out from Tennessee on July 2, 1863, with 2,460 mounted infantrymen, four cannon, and orders to attack Louisville and damage Union supply lines in Kentucky. He chose to cross the Ohio River and raid in Indiana and Ohio. Seizing two steamboats at Brandenburg, he crossed his command over into Indiana. Pursued by converging Union troops and militia, Morgan drove eastward, passing just north of Cincinnati. Attempting to escape back over the river near Pomeroy, he was stopped by a gunboat after only three hundred of his troops had crossed. He finally surrendered his remaining force on July 26 (Dumas Malone, ed., *Dictionary of American Biography* 4:317).

8. Gallipolis, Ohio, is about forty miles upriver from Catlettsburg, Kentucky.

9. Charleston (not "Charlestown"), West Virginia, is on the Kanawha River, which joins the Ohio near Gallipolis.

10. Here McIntire reveals the discrepancy in his stated birth date and the events. Had he been born in 1846, he would have been sixteen in 1860, before the Civil War. Yet his adventures along the Ohio clearly took place after the war.

11. Charleston was the center of a coal mining district, and there were many towns in the area with "coal" as part of their names. McIntire may have meant Coalburgh, up the Kanawha River about fifteen miles from Charleston.

12. Paper money in denominations of less than a dollar were called "shin-plasters," and the term came to mean any money of little value.

Chapter 2. How I Became a Cowboy

1. The distance from Pomeroy to Cincinnati by riverboat is much greater—255 miles, according to *Lloyd's Steamboat Directory and Disasters on the Western Waters,* published in 1856. *Ohio No. 4* was the fourth boat on the river to be named *The Ohio.*

2. The Ohio and Erie Canal, connecting Cleveland on Lake Erie with Portsmouth on the Ohio, a distance of 309 miles, was completed in 1832. The crew of a typical freight-carrying canal boat consisted of a captain (usually the boat owner), a steersman, a bowsman, and a mule driver. Most captains sported distinctive headgear, usually a stovepipe hat, and, on special occasions, some wore military-type uniforms with braid and brass buttons. An entire subculture developed around the boats during the canalboat era. The captains often raised families on the boats and generations of children grew up knowing no home but the tiny rear cabins. Canalboat men were notorious brawlers and fought each other on slight provocation. "At the plodding speed of four miles an hour or less, their job was essentially boring and physical competition between crews helped to relieve the endless monotony" (Jack Gieck, *A Photo Album of Ohio's Canal Era, 1825–1913,* 228). Around the locks saloons sprang up and became hangouts for "canal bad men" who forced themselves onto boats and rode them for days, terrorizing passengers. McIntire's experience on Ohio's rivers and canals provided excellent preparation for the violent times to come in the West.

3. Chillicothe, fifty miles north of Portsmouth, lies on the Scioto River, which formed the southernmost leg of the Ohio and Erie Canal.

4. The Miami and Erie Canal, completed in 1845, was 250 miles in length and connected Cincinnati, on the Ohio, with Toledo, on Lake Erie. It is unlikely that Jeffers took his canal boat west from Portsmouth to Cincinnati; McIntire probably misnamed the Ohio and Erie Canal.

5. The duel McIntire describes took place a decade prior to this. On May 8, 1862, in Bracken County near Dover, Kentucky, a duel was fought between United States Army Colonel Leonidas Metcalfe, son of a former Kentucky governor, and William T. Casto, onetime mayor of Maysville. Metcalfe had jailed Casto, among others, as a Confederate sympathizer, and upon his release, Casto challenged the Union officer. The fight was at sixty yards with Colt's rifles as weapons. Casto was struck near the heart and died within moments; Metcalfe was not injured (Richard H. Collins, *History of Kentucky* 1:102; G. Glenn Clift, *History of Maysville and Mason County* 1:223). It is possible that

McIntire at the age of eight witnessed this duel in the company of his father in 1862, but more likely he heard the story told and retold by canal men and boat hands along the river years later and incorporated the dramatic event into his own history.

6. The expression "shoot the can" does not appear in any of the dictionaries of slang and McIntire's reference is unclear.

7. It may be significant that McIntire held his cockfights "in the basement of a grocery." The elder McIntire was a grocer, and his anger upon discovery of the illicit activity may have stemmed as much from the use of his building as from his son's participation.

8. Evidently, McIntire went back to Brown County to enlist Lyman "Cash" Denny, a childhood friend, in his plans. Lyman was the youngest of the seven children of William and Jane Denny of Brown County. William Denny died before 1870, and by that time all the other children had left home except an older brother who was running the family farm and caring for his aging mother. "Cash" and McIntire were not exactly children when they "ran away from home." McIntire was nineteen, and Denny was eighteen in 1873 (Eighth Census [1860], Brown County, Ohio; Ninth Census [1870], Brown County, Ohio). Characteristically, McIntire does not give the year of his move to Texas, but it appears from the earlier accounts and the subsequent history that it was 1873.

9. McIntire's representation of Dallas as a "straggling village" is inexplicable. He surely must have been impressed by the rapidly growing city. There were over six thousand inhabitants and one hundred stores in the burgeoning town in 1873, according to a handbill entitled "Dallas and Dallas County," published that year. Dallas had been incorporated since 1856 and had a population of almost three thousand as early as 1870. The first Houston & Texas Central train arrived on July 16, 1872 (Darwin Payne, *Dallas: An Illustrated History*, 61; John William Rogers, *The Lusty Texans of Dallas*, 116).

10. Like his description of Dallas, McIntire's assertion that Fort Worth "consisted of one house" is hard to understand. The town had been settled since 1849, had been the seat of Tarrant County since 1860, and was incorporated in 1873, the year McIntire first saw it (Walter Prescott Webb, ed., *The Handbook of Texas* 1:634).

11. Edward S. Terrell, said to be the first white man to pitch a tent on the land which later became Fort Worth, was born in Kentucky in 1812 and would have been sixty-one years old when McIntire met him. Terrell served as city marshal of Fort Worth that year. He later settled in Graham, Young County, where he died in 1905 at the age of ninety-three ("Trails Grown Dim," *Frontier Times* 52 [Aug.–Sept. 1978]: 1).

12. Weatherford, about thirty miles west of Fort Worth, had been incor-

porated since 1858. It was a major freight and stagecoach terminus until the development of the railroads (Webb, ed., *Handbook of Texas* 2:872).

13. The Blackwell House, a two-story frame building with porches at both levels, was on the east side of the square and was being advertised by its owner, Dr. J. W. H. Blackwell, as early as 1858. A dining hall and saloon on the first floor were reportedly the scenes of several gunfights ("Kissin' Kin," by Evlyn Broumley in the *Weatherford Democrat*, November 6, 1988; Evlyn Broumley to RKD, February 23, 1990).

14. James C. Loving, son of pioneer Texas cattleman Oliver Loving, was born June 6, 1836, in Hopkins, Kentucky. He learned the cattle business on his father's ranch in Palo Pinto County, Texas, and drove herds to New Mexico, Kansas, and Colorado after the Civil War. He established a ranch on Dillingham Prairie in Jack County in 1869 and in early 1873 decided to move his operation to Big Lost Valley, about fifteen miles west of Jacksboro. He was in Weatherford looking for ranchhands to work his new spread when McIntire met him (Thomas F. Horton, *History of Jack County*, 84–88). Loving helped found the Texas Cattle Raisers Association, served as the group's first secretary, and held that position until his death in Fort Worth, November 24, 1902 (Webb, ed., *Handbook of Texas* 2:87).

15. Big Lost Valley.

16. Jacksboro, a small town near Fort Richardson, one of the line of forts established by the United States Army to protect settlers on the Texas frontier, had its beginnings in 1855. Originally called Jacksborough, the town became the seat of Jack County in 1858. The name was changed to Jacksboro in 1899 (Webb, ed., *Handbook of Texas* 1:900).

17. Thomas F. Horton, a resident of Jacksboro since 1868, records that two white soldiers from Fort Richardson were killed outside a building in which a number of blacks were holding a dance. The act was reportedly committed by a black man named Charles Copelan. The next morning several white soldiers and a Jacksboro blacksmith named McGinnis went in search of the killer. The blacks, including Copelan, had fled, but the whites, intent on revenge, found one black man named George Mosely and riddled him with bullets. McGinnis was later convicted on charges of accessory to murder, but he broke jail and disappeared. The soldiers were not prosecuted. Horton gives 1874 as the year of this occurrence, but the bodies McIntire remembered seeing outside the dancehall were probably the two dead soldiers (Horton, *Jack County*, 76).

Chapter 3. Life on the Ranch

1. McIntire provides very few dates in his narrative, and it is strange that he specifically includes this one, which is so incorrect. It is evident from a

number of accounts, including the published recollections of R. S. Purdy, who arrived at the Loving ranch with a contingent of Texas Rangers that day, that the incident took place on the tenth of July, 1874. Since the Texas Ranger Frontier Battalion of which Purdy was a member was not formed until June of 1874, his statement is most credible (Horton, *Jack County,* 54; R. S. Purdy, "Fight With Indians at Loving's Ranch," *Frontier Times* 2 [June 1925]: 2).

In his report of July 14, 1874, to Adjutant General William Steele, Major John B. Jones of the Texas Rangers refers to the incident as happening a few days previous (Jones to Steele, July 14, 1874, Adjutant-General's Files, [hereafter A. G. F.], Texas State Library, Austin, Texas).

2. Among the recruits from Jacksboro were John Heath, N. Brumbelow, Ira Cooper, Harry Cooper, and Jack Henson (Horton, *Jack County,* 54).

3. Horton says the fight began early in the morning, as the Indians had slipped into the corral during the night. McIntire and the cowboys were eating breakfast, not dinner (ibid.).

4. This name was probably "Willett" and not "White." J. C. Loving married Mary E. Willett in 1857 and his brother-in-law's name was therefore Willett (ibid., 84).

5. Jack Henson, one of the newly hired hands.

6. All accounts agree on the nature of Heath's wound. Horton wrote that "he was shot in the forehead and the ball came out at the back of his head and brains came out at both front and back." He said that Heath lived more than an hour after being shot but never regained consciousness. Purdy reported that the cowboy had been "pierced through the center of the forehead," and that Ira Cooper caught him and carried him to the ranchhouse, "but he only lived a few minutes" (Horton, *Jack County,* 54; Purdy, "Fighting Indians," 2).

7. "In the fight one of the Indians' horses was captured and the horse was covered with blood" (Horton, *Jack County,* 54). An account of the fight published in 1953 lists the participants "as near as the relator can remember" as "Coon Cooper, Cal Sanders, Ira Cooper, Bill Jay, wagon boss; John Heath, Jones Keith, Nath Brumlow, Jim Loving, Shad Damaron, Tobe Tipton, Henry Wormwood, Buck Cooper, a negro boy who lived with the Coopers; Jim Reagan, Frank Chase, and Crosseyed Bob Carson" (John M. Turner, "Indian Fight in Loving County in 1874," *Frontier Times* 30 [1953]: 236). The names of Jim McIntire or Cash Denny are not mentioned in any of the accounts of the fight.

8. The name is given by Horton as J. K. P. Wright (Horton, *Jack County,* 54).

9. Horton says this incident occurred in 1873 or 1874, but it certainly took place before the fight at the ranchhouse where Heath was killed (ibid.).

10. Willett: see n. 4 above.

11. Although according to McIntire's narrative these horse-stealing stories took place after the July 1874 fight at the Loving ranch, they actually preceded that incident. They were typical of the raids committed by Indians off the reservation during this period; such incidents resulted in the formation of the Frontier Battalion of Texas Rangers. Purdy was a member of one of these newly established companies.

Chapter 4. Indian Atrocities

1. W. R. and J. C. Curtis were cattlemen of the area (Horton, *Jack County*, 85).

2. McIntire is referring to the town of Fort Griffin, in Shackelford County to the southwest of Jack County. This village blossomed in the flatland below the 1867 military post of the same name. The town of Fort Griffin, or "The Flat" as it was sometimes called, was an outfitting point for the buffalo hunters active in the area during the 1870s. It also was renowned for providing the soldiers, hunters, and cattlemen of the surrounding counties with liquor, gambling, and prostitution.

3. Graham is in Young County, about midway between Fort Griffin and Jacksboro.

4. Horton gives these names as W. C. Hunt, Shad Dameron, and J. G. Newcomb (Horton, *Jack County*, 52).

5. McIntire apparently meant Montague County, which, together with Clay County, lies north, not south, of Jack County. The Red River forms the northern boundary of these counties; beyond lay Indian Territory and the reservations.

6. Again McIntire badly confuses various incidents and their sequence. The pursuit of Loving and his cowboys took place on July 12, 1874, only two days after the fight at the Loving ranch, described in the previous chapter. The Indians who attacked the ranch and killed John Heath were a band of marauding Comanches who then moved on (W. S. Nye, *Carbine and Lance: The Story of Old Fort Sill*, 252). On the morning of the twelfth, advance scouts of a large Kiowa war party led by Lone Wolf sighted Loving's cowboys and chased them back to the ranch. This led directly to the Lost Valley Fight that same day between Lone Wolf's Kiowas and the Texas Rangers. McIntire participated in this action which he does not describe until forty pages later, in chapter 7.

7. The atrocities recounted here took place sixteen years previously, long before McIntire went to Texas. Having heard these tales from old Jack County residents, he, intentionally or not, credited the depredations to the Indian raiders of 1874. W. C. Kutch, one of the oldest inhabitants of Jack County, had been in the area and had signed the 1856 petition for establishment of the county; in

1922 he described the Indian attack on the settlers referred to by McIntire. It occurred on April 18, 1858, and the "old gray-haired man and woman" were Kutch's uncle and aunt, Mr. and Mrs. James B. Cambren. Both were slain together with their two oldest sons, and when a "little boy three years old began screaming and crying, they ran a spear down his throat, then speared him twice in the side and killed him." The Indians took another boy as a prisoner but left a seven-year-old girl and her two-year-old brother. The captured boy was later rescued by members of an immigrant train that encountered the Indian party, and the other children were found by neighbors. Tom and Mary Mason were killed the same day by this band of Indians. Kutch did not add the gory details regarding Mrs. Mason's death, saying only, "they shot her down" (Horton, *Jack County*, 33–34).

Chapter 5. Winter on the Ranch

1. As with the county of the same name, McIntire refers to the town of Palo Pinto as "Paliponte."
2. "Willot" was probably the son of the Willotts, Loving's in-laws.

Chapter 6. Hunting Buffalo for Profit

1. McIntire evidently entered into the business of buffalo hunting early in the spring of 1875 after having seen the immense herds which had drifted down into Texas from Kansas and Nebraska for the winter.
2. William C. "Big Bill" Gilson was the first city marshal of Jacksboro after its incorporation in January 1875. However, prior to incorporation the businessmen of Jacksboro, probably hired Gilson as a private policeman to maintain order in the town and protect their property interests. This was a common practice in developing frontier communities. He was "the ideal city marshal," according to T. F. Horton, who described him as "a huge man, cool, brave, quick, powerful, and possessing every element necessary to cope with the toughs who sought to run the town. Gilson took them in all alike and they knew their man well enough to let him alone" (Horton, *Jack County*, 124.) Gilson was later city marshal at Fort Griffin.
3. W. M. D. Lee and A. E. Reynolds were highly successful frontier entrepreneurs who had branched out from lucrative post sutler contracts at several west Texas military camps into many enterprises including freighting, stagecoaching, general store merchandising, Indian trading, ranching, and commerce in buffalo hides (C. Robert Haywood, *Trails South: The Wagon-Road Economy in the Dodge City–Panhandle Region*, 124–125.)
4. "Trails Grown Dim," *Frontier Times* 52 (Aug.–Sept. 1978): 1.

5. Fort Belknap, the military post, had been established on the east bank of the Brazos, some fifteen miles north of the Clear Fork, in 1851. Abandoned at the start of the Civil War, it was reoccupied after the war and was maintained until its final closing in 1876. The nearby village of Belknap was designated county seat of Young County in 1856. It was virtually abandoned during the Civil War and the county records were moved to Jacksboro. Young County was reorganized in 1874, and the town of Graham was selected as the new county seat. Belknap continued as a stage station and maintained its post office, but after the closing of the fort and the relocation of county activities, it never developed as a town. The 1870 census listed sixty-seven inhabitants; by 1880 there were only forty-four (Barbara A. Neal Ledbetter, *Fort Belknap Frontier Saga;* Webb, ed., *Handbook of Texas* 1:140, 620).

6. In 1874 an American team of sharpshooters sponsored by the newly formed National Rifle Association met a rifle team from Ireland in a well-publicized competition at the Association's rifle range at Creedmore, Long Island, New York. The Americans, using breech-loading Sharps and Remington rifles, defeated the Irish, who relied on muzzle-loaders, previously believed to be superior for accuracy. McIntire's rifle was probably a Sharps Model 1874 Sporting Rifle in caliber .44/90, called the "Creedmore" to capitalize on the celebrity of the recent event (Capt. John Houston Craige, *The Practical Book of American Guns,* 87–89; Richard Rattenbury, "Shooting a Stand: Buffalo Rifles on the West Texas Frontier," *Man at Arms 9* [Nov.–Dec. 1987]).

7. This was Fort Richardson; there was no "Fort Jacksboro." McIntire consistently makes this error.

Chapter 7. With the Rangers

1. There are significant discrepancies between McIntire's accounts of his service in the Texas Rangers and the actual Ranger records, which are incomplete and confusing. The "Captain Hamilton" he says he served under was apparently Lt. G. R. Hamilton, who, according to the Ranger muster rolls, served in Company B, Frontier Battalion, from June 1, 1875, until September 30, 1876. The rolls show that McIntire served a total of eleven months and twenty-eight days in Company B between April 1, 1876, and Feb. 28, 1878, under the commands of Hamilton and Lt. G. W. Campbell. The pay records, however, are not in agreement, showing enlistment September 1, 1876, and service through November under Lt. Campbell, a re-enlistment February 14, 1878, and service under Campbell and Capt. June Peak through August 1878. If the pay records are complete, McIntire served a total of nine and a half months. His pay was forty dollars a month, as he states. The two-week pay period February 14–28, 1878, shows McIntire's rank as "corporal," but on all

other records he is listed as a private (Texas Ranger Muster Rolls and Payment Records, A. G. F).

McIntire describes in great detail his adventures with the Rangers in 1874 and 1875, and it is believed he was a member of Company B during this period, although the records do not confirm this. He may have been an unpaid volunteer "Special Ranger," still in the employ of rancher Loving but taken along by the Rangers on their forays because of his knowledge of the country and natural combativeness. Jones' presumed use of these Loving cowboys may explain discrepancies in reports of the number of Rangers engaged in the Lost Valley fight of 1874 (see Allen Lee Hamilton, *Sentinel of the Southern Plains: Fort Richardson and the Northwest Frontier*, 211).

2. This incident occurred more than three years before, not eighteen months as stated by McIntire. On May 18, 1871, a government wagon train en route from Jacksboro to Fort Griffin was attacked by a band of some 150 Indians near Flat Top Mountain and the wagonmaster and six teamsters were killed, and forty-one mules were stolen. Another teamster was wounded but escaped with two others. (H. H. McConnell, "The Massacre of Henry Warren's Train," *Frontier Times* 2 [May 1925]: 16; Ed Carnal, "Reminiscences of a Ranger," *Frontier Times* 1 [December 1923]: 21; Horton, *Jack County*, 39).

3. On May 2, 1874, Governor Richard Coke, acting under authority granted by the Texas legislature, commissioned John B. Jones of Corsicana as a major to command a Frontier Battalion of Texas Rangers for the protection of the state's frontiers. Jones was authorized to establish six companies of seventy-five men each, lettered from A to F, and officered by a captain and first and second lieutenants. By early July Jones had all six companies organized and had joined them in the field. The adjutant general of Texas was William Steele, Jones's boss (Walter Prescott Webb, *The Texas Rangers: A Century of Frontier Defense*, 312).

4. Tom Wilson at this time was acting as a lieutenant in the company of Rangers raised in Palo Pinto County, which McIntire consistently refers to as "Paliponte" County. Wilson served as sheriff of Palo Pinto County, married a daughter of Oliver Loving, and was killed in the line of duty (Mary Whatley Clarke, *The Palo Pinto Story*, 37).

5. Big Tree and Satanta were leaders in the Kiowa attack on the government mule train in 1871. When Satanta later bragged of the massacre at Fort Sill, he was arrested, together with Big Tree and Satank, another Kiowa chieftain, and taken to Texas for trial. Satank was killed en route by a guard, and Satanta and Big Tree were sentenced to death. Later the sentence was reduced to life imprisonment, and they were locked up at the state prison at Huntsville. In October 1873, Satanta and Big Tree were paroled by Governor Edmund J. Davis, a decision that was widely condemned. The two chiefs were blamed for

Indian attacks occurring the following year. The leader of the Kiowa raiders in July 1874, however, was Lone Wolf, who sought revenge for a humiliating defeat suffered by the Indians at the hands of a determined little band of buffalo hunters at the Battle of Adobe Walls in the Panhandle the previous month (Nye, *Carbine and Lance*, 140–147, 168, 191–200).

6. Rangers W. A. Glass and George Moore were wounded (Jones to Steele, July 14, 1874, A. G. F.). Moore was wounded so severely below the knee that he was crippled the rest of his life, according to Walter M. Robertson, who was a member of Captain Stephens' company (Walter M. Robertson, "The Loss [*sic*] Valley Fight," *Frontier Times* 7 [December 1929]: 100–104).

7. Jones gives this name as Lee Corn (Jones to Steele, July 14, 1874. A. G. F.).

8. The names of the men who went for water have been given as D. W. "Dave" Bailey and M. W. "Mel" Porter (ibid.; Cora Melton Cross, "Ira Long, Cowboy and Texas Ranger," *Frontier Times* 8 [October 1930]: 26).

9. Said Ed Carnal, who was a Ranger participant in this action: "Poor fellow! There was little of him left. His clothing was all gone and his body was terribly mutilated. He had been lanced and cut with Bowie knives until it was with difficulty one could recognize the remains as being those of a human. Even his head had been taken entirely away" (Carnal, "Reminiscences," 23). But Carnal made no mention of cannibalism by the Indians. Robertson said that Bailey's remains were "a terrible sight, having been horribly mutilated, and he had been scalped. Fourteen or fifteen arrows were taken from his body" (Robertson, "The Loss [*sic*] Valley Fight," 103). He did not explain how he knew the ranger had been scalped if his head had been removed.

Hunting Horse, one of the Kiowas who was in the battle, in an interview with Capt. W. S. Nye, said,

When I got to the place where they had killed the other ranger [Bailey], I learned that Dohauson had thrust him off his horse with a spear, but that Mamaday-te had made first coup by touching him with his hand. Lone Wolf and Mamaday-te and everybody was there. Lone Wolf got off his horse and chopped the man's head to pieces with his brass hatchet-pipe. Then he took out his butcher knife and cut open the man's bowels. Everyone who wanted to shot arrows into it or poked it with their lances. (Nye, *Carbine and Lance*, 257).

The parents of Billy Glass found his burial site and removed his remains later, but Bailey's body "still lies there unmarked and uncared for" (Cross, "Ira Long," 27).

10. Carnal was more charitable toward the black troops:

We then resumed our efforts to find the main trail of the Indians, as we were very anxious to get those troops on it, but [there were] so many trails, all leading in different directions, that we found it impossible. This was one of their favorite methods after an attack . . . to scatter in all directions, traveling possibly for miles paralleling each other but finally all trails converging at a given point previously agreed upon. . . . We scouted for the greater part of the day trying to locate this trail for the black troops with no success what ever. (Carnal, "Reminiscences," 23)

11. As evidenced by all accounts other than McIntire's, this action took place on July 12, 1874, two days after the Indian fight at Loving's ranch described by McIntire in Chapter 3.

Ida Lasater Huckabay, in her history of Jack County, says that the Rangers stationed near Jacksboro in 1874 "terrorized the citizens." The company, she says, was composed "chiefly of men from other States who had come west to grow up with the country," an apt description of Jim McIntire, at least (Ida Lasater Huckabay, *Ninety-four Years in Jack County, 1854–1948*, 142).

12. The arrest of Satanta and Big Tree for violation of their parole was directed on October 30, 1874, by Gen. Philip Sheridan, and a week later Satanta was returned to Huntsville. Four years later he committed suicide by diving into a brick wall from a second-floor window. Big Tree was not apprehended and lived in Indian Territory until November 13, 1929, when he died at Anadarko, Oklahoma (Horton, *Jack County*, 46).

13. The incident McIntire now describes took place the following year, on May 8, 1875 (Jones to Steele, May 9, 1875, A. G. F).

14. Ira Long, born in Indiana in 1842 and raised in Missouri, was commissioned a lieutenant in the Confederate Army at the age of nineteen and was wounded seriously at the battle of Mansfield. After the war he settled in Wise County, Texas, and was appointed lieutenant of a company of Rangers raised there by Major Jones (Cross, "Ira Long," 22–25); Horton, *Jack County*, 52). Celebrated frontier lawman Jeff Milton served under Long a few years later and described him as "one of the most conscientious and fearless men" he ever knew: "He wa'n't afraid of anybody. He could figure in his head faster than any man in the country, and he couldn't read or write" (J. Evetts Haley, *Jeff Milton: A Good Man With a Gun*, 31).

15. The woman "made every effort to surrender, making overtures to the rangers, exposing her breasts to show that she was a woman," but the Rangers, hardened by first-hand knowledge of some of the atrocities committed by the Indians, shot her in cold blood. She "appeared to be beautiful, quite young and very attractive, possessing every feature of being of the white race, perhaps a half-breed, or possibly a white woman captured in early childhood, reared by the Indians, and exposed to wind and weather until very dark in complexion. However, the writer is inclined to the opinion that she was a white woman, otherwise she would not have made such strenuous efforts at surrender, something a full-blood Indian was never, in my experience, known to do" (Horton, *Jack County*, 56).

16. Long later described this hand-to-hand fight: "I recall how thankful I was that I was big and brawny and strong and then we closed. I had never then, nor have I since, seen such strength and agility as that Indian possessed. When I threw him off in a grapple, he bounced like a rubber ball. And he used his gunstock as skillfully as I did mine" (Cross, "Ira Long," 28).

17. The escaped Indian was mounted on a horse of Oliver Loving, son of the ranch owner. It was "a small horse but strong and very fleet and of great endurance" (Horton, *Jack County*, 56.)

18. Since the woman was apparently partly white, and the man McIntire refers to as a "renegade white man" had curly, auburn hair, there was some talk that the marauders were not Indians at all, but whites disguised as Indians. To settle the point, soldiers from Fort Richardson came out to the site, cut the heads from the dead, preserved them in jars of alcohol, and sent them off to Washington. Ranger Bailey's mutilation had been effectively avenged. Nye says the party was comprised of Comanches off the reservation on a horse-stealing expedition, and he identifies the auburn-haired brave as Ay-cufty, which means "Reddish." The leader was Isa-toho (Black Coyote) and the woman was his wife (Nye, *Carbine and Lance*, 303–304).

19. McIntire may be confusing "Black Coyote" and his wife, the Comanches the Rangers had slain, with "Black Crow" and his wife.

20. Milton J. Yarberry was a twenty-six-year-old drifter who had fled Sharp County, Arkansas, with a price on his head after a killing. He was reported to have ridden in a rustler gang in the Fort Smith area with Dave Rudabaugh and Mysterious Dave Mather, two hard cases McIntire would run up against later. After being implicated in a killing at Fort Smith and another at Texarkana, Yarberry joined the Rangers in Jack County (R. K. DeArment, "The Blood-Spattered Trail of Milton J. Yarberry," *Old West* 22 [Fall 1985]: 8–14).

21. Yarberry was initially appointed but was later elected to the position of constable at Albuquerque. He killed two men during his brief tenure, and for the second murder he was given the death penalty. He was hanged at Albuquerque, February 9, 1883, by the "jerk" method, that is, he was jerked into the air by a noose around his neck when a weight attached to the other end of the rope was dropped (ibid.).

Chapter 8. Weeding Out the Outlaws

1. Major Jones reported to the Texas legislature that the Rangers during the year 1875 had "rendered assistance to the civil authorities in maintaining law and suppression of crime," and had "broken up several organizations of outlaws and fugitives from justice." They had been involved in six fights with

outlaws and had "turned over to the civil authorities about one hundred fugitives from justice" (Report quoted in Jerry Sinise, *George Washington Arrington: Civil War Spy, Texas Ranger, Sheriff and Rancher,* 19).

2. On August 26, 1876, William G. England (not Meeks), a Methodist minister, his wife, and two step-children were murdered in Montague County. The victims were shot by three intruders. England's throat was also cut, a circumstance leading to early newspaper reports that the family had been slain with knives *(Galveston Daily News,* September 2, 1876). Arrested by Sheriff Lee N. Perkins and charged with the murders were Ben Krebs, aged 48, James Preston, aged 52, and 16-year-old A. K. Taylor (Case file, A. G. F., Texas State Archives).

3. On December 10, 1876, Lt. G. W. Campbell, a detachment of Rangers, and Sheriff Perkins took Krebs, Preston, Taylor, and three other prisoners, George Brown, Sr., George Brown, Jr., and Jesse Brown, to the Cooke County jail in Gainesville, for safekeeping and to await trial (Report of Lt. G. W. Campbell, for period December 1 to December 15, 1876, A. G. F.). The Browns were considered desperate characters but were held on other charges and had no connection to the England family murder case *(Galveston Daily News,* August 15, 1876).

4. Krebs, Preston, and Taylor were tried and convicted of the murder of the England family. The two older men were sentenced to hang; Taylor, due to his youth, was given a life sentence. After all appeals were exhausted, Governor Oran M. Roberts commuted the death sentences to life imprisonment. Taylor died in prison later that year, and Krebs and Preston were finally pardoned by Governor James S. Hogg in 1895 (Case File, A. G. F., Texas State Archives.)

5. Lee N. Perkins served as sheriff of Montague County from February 15, 1876, until November 5, 1878 (Sammy Tise, *Texas County Sheriffs,* 379).

6. "Open warfare brought Texas Rangers hurrying to Griffin. Captain [*sic*] G. W. Campbell headed the twenty-five or thirty Rangers as in a column of twos they rode down Griffin's dusty street" (Carl Coke Rister, *Fort Griffin on the Texas Frontier,* 157).

7. Night riders and vigilantes calling themselves "Regulators" and opposing groups labeled "Moderators" had appeared on the frontier in as widely dispersed areas as California, Iowa, and Texas. Often, they had come into violent conflict. In Texas the most notable collision of factions bearing these names occurred in the eastern part of the state in the 1840s (Wayne Gard, *Frontier Justice,* 22–39). There were, as McIntire indicates, two groups in violent contention at Fort Griffin, but they did not call themselves by these names. "The settlers of Fort Griffin country found themselves aligned, actually or in sympathy, with one or the other of two hostile groups," wrote Carl Rister. "The vigilance committee was supported by those seeking to stamp out lawlessness

and the rival group by thieves, gamblers, prostitutes, and ne'er-do-wells. There could be no middle ground" (Rister, *Fort Griffin*, 157). The vigilantes were known in Shackelford County as the "Tin Hat Band Brigade," or simply, "Tin Hats" (Huckabay, *Ninety-Four Years*, 148). The April 13, 1878, report of Lt. G. W. Campbell of the Rangers refers to them as the "bloodthirsty and cutthroat 'Tin Hat' committee" (quoted in Ed Bartholomew, *Wyatt Earp: the Untold Story*, 228). The origin of the "Tin Hat" term is not known.

8. John Larn (not Long) was a handsome, well-spoken Alabaman who had arrived at Fort Griffin about 1870 and taken employment as foreman for Joe Matthews, a leading rancher of Shackelford County. Although stories circulated that Larn had an unsavory past and had killed a man or two, he was generally well liked; within a short time he had married Matthews' daughter, established a ranch of his own, and seemed on his way to a prosperous respectability. In 1876 he was elected sheriff and took on as deputy a cold-eyed gunman named John Selman. These two were prominent members of the "Tin Hat" vigilance committee, an organization accused by its enemies of thievery and murder for personal gain. On March 7, 1877, Larn resigned his office, and William Cruger was appointed to succeed him.

9. Larn and Selman continued their night-riding activities and on the night of June 22, 1878, a posse headed by Sheriff Cruger rode to Larn's ranch and arrested him. He was taken to Albany, shackled, and placed in a shack that served as the Shackelford County jail. That night, nine masked men (or eleven, or twenty—reports vary) entered the building, held jailor John Poe at gunpoint, and riddled Larn with bullets. The posse also searched for Selman, but he was alerted and escaped in the night (Leon Metz, *John Selman: Texas Gunfighter*, 82–89).

10. There is little to support this story. Contrary to his assertion that Gilson was a friend of Larn's and feared for his own life after the lynching, Gilson has been named as one of the men who killed the former sheriff (Metz, *John Selman*, 86). Ida Huckabay, Jack County historian, provides McIntire's tale tenuous corroboration when she writes that Bill Gilson was later killed at Fort Griffin because "it appeared that 'Big Bill' knew too much about the Tin Hat Band Brigade and some of the members were afraid he would, or had, "blown" on them" (Huckabay, *Ninety-Four Years*, 148), but she diminishes her credibility by citing the *Fort Griffith* (sic) *Echo* of July 5, 1878. The *Fort Griffin Echo* was not established until January 4, 1879 (Rister, *Fort Griffin*, 160). Gilson drifted on to Sweetwater, Nolan County, where he served as city marshal in 1881–1882. He was reportedly killed there by a man named Jim Cooksey (Rollie Burns, "Reminiscence of 56 Years").

11. The death of Larn and the disappearance of John Selman from the area

brought an end to the vigilante war in Shackelford County. Within two months, Lt. G. W. Arrington, who in July replaced Lieutenant Campbell as head of the Rangers at Griffin, could report to Major Jones that everything was quiet and that although "at one time nearly everybody belonged to the mob . . . the good men are now satisfied that law and order can be maintained without lynch law . . ." (quoted in C. L. Sonnichsen, *I'll Die Before I'll Run: The Story of the Great Feuds of Texas*, 165–166).

12. Here, again, McIntire has his sequence of events wrong. The Shackelford County Rangers' participation in the Sam Bass hunt took place in May 1878, a month before the arrest and lynching of John Larn. The celebrated outlaw Sam Bass, like Jim McIntire, was a Midwesterner who had drifted to Texas at the age of nineteen seeking adventure. Born in Indiana in 1851, he arrived in Denton, Texas, in 1870. In 1876 he helped drive a herd of cattle to the boomtown of Deadwood, Dakota Territory, where he turned to outlawry. He led a gang in several stagecoach holdups before making a major heist, the looting of a Union Pacific train near Big Springs, Nebraska, of more than sixty thousand dollars. Back in Texas, the Bass gang committed a series of holdups in the Dallas area that precipitated a massive manhunt involving state, county, and municipal officers (Wayne Gard, *Sam Bass*, passim; Paula Reed and Grover Ted Tate, *The Tenderfoot Bandits, Sam Bass and Joel Collins: Their Lives and Hard Times*, passim).

13. Ioni Creek in Palo Pinto County. Officers had traced the Bass gang to this area and on May 26 Lieutenant Campbell and Corporal Jack Smith led a force of nineteen Rangers from Shackelford County to help in the manhunt (Reed and Tate, *Tenderfoot Bandits*, 181).

14. In spite of the efforts by some fifty manhunters to trap him, Bass eluded them all and remained free for six more weeks until cornered and killed by Texas Rangers at Round Rock on July 19, 1878 (Reed and Tate, *Tenderfoot Bandits*, 193–229).

15. McIntire continues to allude to "Captain Hamilton," when the officer he means is Lt. G. W. Campbell. Lieutenant Arrington replaced Campbell in July 1878 (Rister, *Fort Griffin*, 157).

16. Junius "June" Peak, a professional peace officer of Dallas, was enlisted by Major Jones in April 1878 to organize a detachment of Company B of the Frontier Battalion for the express purpose of hunting down the Sam Bass gang. Peak was a Confederate veteran and had been a member of Morgan's Raiders, who had fought through McIntire's Ohio country in 1863 (Reed and Tate, *Tenderfoot Bandits*, 152–153). Ranger payment records show that McIntire was a member of Captain June Peak's company until the end of August 1878.

Chapter 9. Running a Saloon in Texas

1. Newton F. Locke was a Southerner, son of an Alabaman who died for
the Confederate cause in the Civil War. Born near Selma on January 13, 1853,
he went to Texas at the age of twenty-one and worked in a Dallas store for a
year. In 1875 he took a job in a store at Jacksboro, where he probably first met
McIntire. He enlisted in Company B, Frontier Battalion of the Texas Rangers,
on April 1, 1876, the same day as McIntire (Texas Ranger Muster Rolls,
A. G. F.; B. B. Paddock, *A Twentieth Century History and Biographical Record of North and West Texas*, 298).

2. "A spool of thread or a package of needles brought twenty-five cents.
A drink of whiskey or a cigar sold for a quarter. A dime or five-cent piece was
unknown," wrote George Curry of conditions at Sweetwater, Wheeler County,
another frontier village developing at this time (H. B. Hening, ed., *George Curry, 1861–1947: An Autobiography*, 10).

3. Brothers Eugene, Alonzo, and Hiram Millett in 1875 joined with cattlemen Seth Mabry, John O. DeWees, and James F. Ellison in the largest northern cattle drive on record. In 1874 they had established a ranch in Baylor
County and were among the most successful cattlemen of the period, but they
were notorious for employing hard-case cowboys. A. P. Black, who worked for
the Milletts in the 1880s, called the ranch "one of the toughest spots this side
of Hell. . . . When the Millets run the spread there wasn't anybody but a rustler
or gunman could get work with them. . . . The Millets were a tough outfit
straight through and hired the toughest bunch of men I ever ran up against"
(A. P. "Ott" Black, *The End of the Long Horn Trail*, 13, 15).

4. Since McIntire was in the Rangers until the end of August, this incident probably took place in September 1878.

5. The winter of 1878–1879.

6. In 1875 Fort Elliott was built on Sweetwater Creek in the eastern section of the Texas Panhandle; a town, first called Hidetown and later Sweetwater,
grew up near the fort. To avoid confusion with the already established post
office at Sweetwater, Nolan County, the name was changed in 1879 to Mobeetie, the Indian name for Sweetwater. That year brought a post office and the seat
of Wheeler County to the town and also brought McIntire and Locke, who
recognized the growth potential signaled by the changes (Webb, ed., *Handbook of Texas*, 2:220; L. F. Sheffy, "Old Mobeetie—The Capital of the Panhandle," *The West Texas Historical Yearbook* 6 [June 1930]: 5).

7. Henry Fleming, an early resident, opened a two-room stone building
as a saloon during the "Hidetown" period when the town was composed primarily of buffalo hunters' shanties made of hides. Fleming's structure had "ceilings so high they could not be reached by standing on a chair and long, narrow

windows high enough from the ground to afford excellent protection from the flying lead of rowdy passersby" (Glenn Shirley, *Temple Houston: Lawyer With a Gun,* 50).

Temple Houston, attorney and son of Sam Houston, arrived in Mobeetie in early 1881 to assume office as district attorney for the Thirty-fifth Judicial District of Texas. He found Sheriff Fleming to be "a tall Irishman, a professional saloon-keeper and gambler of the Hidetown days, but a man of strength and purpose whose word was as good as his marksmanship" (ibid., 51).

Fleming took office as sheriff at the first Wheeler County elections, held on April 12, 1879. Curiously, the *Dodge City Times* of April 26, 1879, in a column entitled "Jottings from the Pan-Handle," reported that "The Wheeling [*sic*] county election is over. . . . The following are the names of the officers elected: County Commissioners, John Donley [*sic*] and J. McIntire. . . ." However, the county records show the first county commissioners elected were John Donely, J. W. Huselby, George A. Montgomery, and Benjamin Williams (William C. Perkins, *A History of Wheeler County, Texas,* 57).

The first county clerk was A. D. "Frosty" Tomb, who, like McIntire, must have been a salty character. Fleming, Tomb, and McIntire were singled out for mention as leading members of the sporting crowd by a chronicler of the town: "[Mobeetie] could not have been without its professional gamblers and its noted women . . . , such institutions as Feather Hill [the red-light district] and such characters as Mother Lemly, Dolly Varden, Frosty Toombes and James McIntire. Even Sheriff Henry Fleming was shrewd enough at cards to win a herd of eight hundred cattle in one night at the gambling tables" (Sheffy, "Old Mobeetie," 13).

Rancher Charles Goodnight believed "that the intention of the county organization was to prevent law and order rather than to enforce it." Although one hundred and fifty qualified voters were necessary for legal organization, it was doubtful there were that many in the entire Panhandle. Those that were there were mostly "gamblers, dance-hall people, and buffalo hunters, many of whom bore such names, if the District Court Minutes are trustworthy, as Butcher Knife Bill, Feather Stone Jones, Matilda Wave, Frog Mouth Annie, and Fly Speck" (J. Evetts Haley, *Charles Goodnight: Cowman and Plainsman,* 358–359). In September 1879 one of the dancehall girls, Belle Hines, filed charges against Jim McIntire for "using obscene language" and being "loud and vociferous in her presence," a ludicrous indictment (Sallie B. Harris, *Hide-Town in the Texas Panhandle,* 35–36). In the fall of 1879 McIntire and Locke served together on a jury in a civil case (Porter, *Memory Cups,* 41).

8. On March 9, 1881, N. F. Locke married; he remained in Mobeetie for fifteen years. In 1884 he was elected clerk of the county and district courts and held the post for eight years. He left Wheeler County in 1894 and settled at

Miami, in Roberts County, where he established a successful mercantile firm,
N. F. Locke and Son, and engaged in ranching. He served a term as treasurer
of Roberts County and two terms as county judge, 1902–1906. He died at
Miami on April 27, 1939 (Harris, *Hide Town*, 80; Paddock, *Biographical Record*,
298–299; *Austin American*, April 28, 1939).

9. McIntire does not mention an encounter he had with outlaws in June
1879 that prompted him to make a sworn statement before County Attorney
Moses Wiley on the thirtieth of that month, in which he expressed his concern
in a rather remarkable document:

On or about the 15th day of June A. D. 1879 I was en route from Fort Dodge, Kansas, to
Fort Elliott, Texas. Near Tuscosa [Tascosa] on the Canadian river, my camp was visited
by a party of men about 8 or 10 in number. They seemed to be headed by a man whom I
knew at Fort Griffin by name of A. L. Mont, commonly called "Long John," now going
by the name of "Jim." He is under indictment in Shackleford County for killing Virgil
Hewey and a colored soldier of the 10th [Cavalry] at Fort Griffin. Among the crowd was
a man said to be brother of Long John, and known by name of "Harry" in Ft. Griffin;
also Billy Smith, charged with stealing one gray horse from Pete Haverty in Fort Griffin.
I did not know any of the rest of the men. They were well armed; Long John told me to
tell anybody that knew them that they had two six shooters and brand new Winchesters
and plenty of boys with them. As I had to stand in with them for the time being, they told
me that if I wanted to come to them, to come from Fort Griffin to Devil's river and there
inquire for Buck Smith or Long John and I would be alright. Long John told me that Buck
Smith is the alias now worn by John Silliman [Selman]. [He] showed me alias names of
men belonging to Silliman's gang on paper; they have adopted names of women, such as
Annie, Sue, etc. Long had this paper from Silliman as an introduction or voucher of who
I was. Said that Silliman was up above at the 'other plaza.' [He] did not explain where
this place was, but gave me the impression that he was not far off.

Long John gave me to understand that in the whole crowd there were about one
hundred and seventy-five men under command of John Silliman, ranging from the Canadian river to Devil's river. Long John had plenty of money and said that "We—," then,
correcting himself, said, "The boys took in a bank the other day in New Mexico and
raised about $15,000.00." They were poorly mounted and John said they were going to
take in a bunch of horses soon. He talked of coming down here with the whole party. He
made inquiries about the County organization, the number of people here, and the number
of troops at the Post at Fort Elliott. I told him that the County was organized. He then
said that he had intended to come down here but that now he would not do it. He told me
of numbers of persons whose names I knew, while a member of the ranger company, for
whom rewards were offered. I cannot say how many men were in the crowd at Tuscosa,
but there were about ten came to my camp. I think, however, that there was a large
number; have heard that as many as seventy-five were there with Silliman near there.
They were making loud threats against Fort Griffin people. . . . Silliman's brother, Tom,
is with them and known as "Tom Cat." John Gross is with them under an alias that I do
not remember. (Sworn Statement of James McIntire before Moses Wiley, June 30, 1879,
Research Center, Panhandle-Plains Historical Museum, Canyon, Texas)

County Attorney Wiley shared McIntire's concern and the next day penned
a letter to Major John B. Jones of the Texas Rangers:

Enclosed herewith find the affidavit of James McIntire. This man is perhaps as well known to yourself as to me. He served a long time in one of the ranger companies and says that he has been with you on several expeditions. He is generally considered a very reliable man. You no doubt know the character of the principal men mentioned in his statement, and can judge of the probability of their executing their threats.

I have reported the matter to the commanding officer, Fort Elliott. It seems that the present laws of Congress forbid the U.S. Army from co-operating with the State civil officers, so that at present the Comdg. officer can do nothing but defend the Gov't property. No one here seems to think that Silliman will venture to attack the [Military]. Probably not—but if attempted, and skill used, the chances are that the attack would be a success, and this success in supplying arms and horses, would soon cause their force to swell to such numbers that nothing short of an army could subdue them. Would the Governor's or President's proclamation, if it could be obtained against these outlaws, serve to authorize the co-operation of the [military] and civil authorities against the outlaws? It is impossible to say where or at what point they will strike, but when as many desperadoes as they have are banded together for the express purpose of outlawry and depredations, it is probable that they will accomplish something startling. And, occupying as they do the interior lines of communication, they can readily concentrate upon any given point on the frontier, which forms a circle around them.

The whole matter is respectfully submitted to your consideration with the hope that your earnest attention will be given to this, to us, important matter.

[Postscript:] McIntire is very anxious that his name should be kept secret, and is very solicitous that you should suppress the use of it in any public manner. It is for that reason the affidavit is made before me instead of the County Clerk. . . . [McIntire is not] willing that there should be any one else here knowing to the affidavit as it might cost him his life. (Moses Wiley to John B. Jones, July 1, 1879, Research Center, Panhandle-Plains Historical Museum, Canyon, Texas)

"Long John," the outlaw McIntire met on the Canadian, was John Longhurst, also known as John Long, J. J. Mont, John Longmont, and Frank Roberts. His pal "John Silliman" was the John Larn cohort, John Selman, who had barely escaped the wrath of the Fort Griffin vigilantes. Selman had ridden into New Mexico in time to get involved in the Lincoln County War troubles, and then formed a gang called the "Wrestlers" or "Rustlers" which seized the opportunity provided by the war's chaos to pillage, rape, and terrorize the countryside. Shortly after McIntire's report, Long disappeared from the area, reportedly slain by a man named Trujillo; Selman almost died from a bout with black smallpox; and other gang members drifted off on different trails (R. K. DeArment, "The Great Outlaw Confederacy," *True West* 37 [Sept. 1990]: 14–19; Metz, *John Selman*, 112; Jeff Burton, ed., *Portraits in Gunsmoke*, 49; Pat Garrett, *The Authentic Life of Billy the Kid*, 80).

It is significant that McIntire was on his way from "Fort Dodge" (i.e., Dodge City) to "Fort Elliott" (i.e., Mobeetie) on June 15. Three days before, on June 12, 1879, W. B. "Bat" Masterson, sheriff of Ford County, Kansas, arrived back in Dodge from Colorado. He had gone to Pueblo a few days before with a force of fifty gunmen to defend the interests of the Atchison, Topeka and

Santa Fe Railroad in its dispute with the Denver and Rio Grande Railroad over
the right of way to the silver mines at Leadville in the so-called "Royal Gorge
War." It is highly likely that McIntire served as one of Masterson's recruits in
that war, joining the likes of Ben Thompson, J. H. "Doc" Holliday, Kinch
Riley, George Goodell, and John Joshua Webb, gunmen all *(Dodge City
Times,* June 14, 1879; Robert K. DeArment, *Bat Masterson: The Man and the
Legend,* 150).

10. With the organization of Wheeler County in 1879, Sheriff Fleming
became responsible for twenty-six other Panhandle counties. His jurisdiction
"embraced the territory extending from No Man's Land on the north and the
New Mexico line on the west to its intersection with about the thirty-fourth
parallel, and extending from that point east to the one hundredth meridian. This
was almost an empire within itself. It was larger than the state of Vermont,
almost as large as the states of Maryland and Massachusetts combined, and was
more than ten times the size of the state of Rhode Island" (Sheffy, "Old Mobeetie," 5–6).

11. Contemporary accounts identify the federal officer in charge of this
operation as "Col. Norton, U.S. Marshal for the Northern District of Texas"
(Dodge City Times, November 29, 1879). This district was created on February
2, 1879, and A. B. Norton was appointed U.S. marshal in charge on April 2.
His raid into Wheeler County in November of that year evidently gained him
no distinction; he was removed from office in 1882 (Robert R. Ernst [Research
Consultant, U.S. Marshal's Service] to RKD, September 25, 1989).

Among the officers with Norton were deputy U.S. marshals Walter Johnson of Dallas and Timothy Isaiah "Longhaired Jim" Courtright of Fort Worth.
The name of Courtright, who had been city marshal at Fort Worth since 1876,
does not appear in contemporary reports of this incident, and his participation
is not mentioned by his various biographers (F. Stanley, *Jim Courtright: Two
Gun Marshal of Fort Worth;* Cunningham, *Triggernometry,* 203–217). McIntire, however, would later be intimately associated with Courtright and it seems
highly unlikely he could have mistaken another man for him. Henry Ossian
Flipper was born at Thomasville, Georgia, March 21, 1856, of slave parents.
He was the first black cadet at West Point, from which he was graduated in 1877
to become the first black commissioned officer in the United States Army. At
the time of this incident he was assigned to the Tenth Cavalry stationed at Fort
Sill (Barry C. Johnson [ed.], *"Ho, For the Great West!"* 133–135).

12. Tom Riley, like McIntire, was a Mobeetie saloonman (Shirley, *Temple
Houston,* 45). The *Dodge City Times* of November 8, 1879, referenced "a St.
Louis dispatch" reporting "a good deal of feeling" in Wheeler County "owing
to the arrest of persons by the United States Deputy Marshals, on blank warrants, filled up to suit the cases." U.S. Marshal Norton had arrived from Dallas

with the blank warrants to arrest Wheeler County residents suspected of selling tobacco without a license and dodging federal tax. It was common practice for ranch owners, as a convenience, to maintain a stock of personal items, including tobacco, for sale to their cowboys. Norton soon rounded up more than a dozen and brought them to Mobeetie for trial before Judge Emanuel Dubbs. When Dubbs, in sympathy with the accused, discharged the cases, Marshal Norton angrily arrested them again, together with all the county officials he could find, and jailed the whole crowd at Fort Elliott. Gravis Leach, later a judge at Mobeetie, wrote that there were a total of thirty-five men locked up (James M. Oswald, "History of Fort Elliott," *Panhandle-Plains Historical Review* 32 [1959]: 40; Harris, *Hide Town*, 25).

13. Ira Rinehart had been an early arrival at Tascosa, another new Panhandle town, lying one hundred miles west of Mobeetie on the Canadian River. A German Jew and former sheriff at Elizabethtown, New Mexico, Rinehart, in partnership with G. J. Howard, opened a general store in Tascosa and sold drugs and patent medicines as well as many other items of merchandise (John L. McCarty, *Maverick Town: The Story of Old Tascosa*, 53).

14. Capt. Nicolas Nolan, post commander at Fort Elliott, had acceded to Marshal Norton's request to jail the prisoners pending clarification of the legal issues, but during the night Lieutenant Flipper took the arrested men out of the guardhouse, loaded them into a wagon, and started for Indian Territory. McIntire's version of the affair (agreed to by Gravis Leach) alleges that this move was in concert with the federal officers; but other sources say that as Flipper tried to rescue the accused, the marshals overtook them. McIntire indicates that only he and Tom Riley stopped the midnight exodus, but Leach says that there was a posse of fifteen men including Judge Dubbs, Sheriff Fleming, and Riley; he does not mention McIntire.

Marshal Norton later escorted Judge Dubbs, Captain Nolan, and Lieutenant Flipper to Dallas, where the military officers were tried and fined one thousand dollars each for interfering in the legal process. Dubbs was released without penalty and Marshal Norton was reprimanded (Oswald, "Fort Elliott," 41; Harris, *Hide Town*, 25–27). "The parties who were arrested in the Pan Handle for alleged violation of the revenue laws and resisting officers have been discharged, the grand jury failing to find a true bill, at its sitting in Dallas," said the *Dodge City Times* of December 20. A week later the paper reported that "R. [Ira] Rinehart, of Tuscosa, Texas, is on his return from Dallas. The arrest of parties in the Pan Handle caused a great deal of indignation; and now the U.S. Marshal and his assistants are catching it" (December 27, 1879).

15. Flipper was not court-martialled over this incident. He subsequently served with distinction in the campaign against the bands of Mimbres Apache chief Victorio in west Texas the following year. Later he was given responsi-

bility for the commissary at Fort Davis. When discrepancies were found in his financial records, he was court-martialled and dismissed from the army June 30, 1882, making him the first black officer to be cashiered. He became a successful civil and mining engineer and was active in mining ventures in Mexico and Central America. He was assistant to the secretary of the interior in 1922–1923. Returning to Georgia, his birthplace, in 1931, he lived there until his death, May 3, 1940 (Johnson [ed.], *"Ho! For the Great West,"* 133–224; Dan L. Thrapp, *Encyclopedia of Frontier Biography* 1:502).

16. The name of Wyatt Earp is, of course, one of the most famous in the lexicon of popular Western figures. A widely read biography by Stuart N. Lake (*Wyatt Earp, Frontier Marshal* [Boston and New York: Houghton Mifflin Co., 1931]) depicted Earp as an absolutely fearless, incorruptible defender of truth and right, the paragon of frontier lawmen. This characterization has been reinforced by innumerable books, magazines, motion pictures, and television shows. But in 1902 when McIntire published his book, Wyatt Earp was virtually unknown outside of the few frontier towns in which he operated, and the name was not dropped due to a high recognition value. Mysterious Dave Mather was a contemporary of Earp in Dodge City and, like Earp, was a professional gambler, gunman, and sometime law officer.

It is reported that Mather and Earp claimed the bricks came from a cache of Spanish gold hidden by early-day priests and were being offered only to finance an expedition to secure the balance of the treasure. The date of the Mather-Earp invasion of Mobeetie is given as September 3, 1878 (Colin Rickards, *Mysterious Dave Mather,* 6). However, it is clear from a story in the *Dodge City Times* of September 9, 1878, that Earp was in Dodge at that time. It is known that Earp did travel extensively in Texas in late 1877 and early 1878, arriving back at Dodge City on May 8, 1878. Mather's movements are unknown for this time and possibly this was when the two were peddling gold bricks. According to McIntire's account, however, he did not settle in Mobeetie until the spring of 1879 and did not become a deputy sheriff until the fall of that year. If the confrontation with Mather and Earp occurred during Earp's lengthy Texas sojourn of 1877–78, McIntire was acting as a Texas Ranger, not as an officer of Wheeler County.

17. No record has yet been uncovered of such an arrest. Wyatt Earp left Dodge City in September 1879, stopped briefly in Las Vegas, New Mexico, and continued on to Tombstone, Arizona, where he played a prominent role in that town's sanguinary history. He later traveled the West as a professional gambler and invested in various mining ventures. He died in Los Angeles, California, January 13, 1929.

18. McIntire had known John W. Poe, a twenty-nine-year-old native of Kentucky, on the buffalo ranges and at Fort Griffin, where Poe had been town

marshal. Poe came to Mobeetie about the same time as McIntire and was employed by the Canadian River Cattle Association to protect their interests in the area. In New Mexico Poe later served as a deputy under Lincoln County Sheriff Pat Garrett and was with him on July 14, 1881, when Garrett killed the notorious outlaw Billy the Kid Bonney (who, as McIntire must have known, was not Hispanic) at Fort Sumner. He succeeded Garrett as sheriff of Lincoln County and served two terms. In 1900 he established the Citizens' Bank of Roswell, referred to by McIntire, and died in that city in 1923 (Sophie Poe, *Buckboard Days*, 17–287; William A. Keleher, *Violence in Lincoln County*, 348–49).

19. According to his wife, Poe followed one fugitive from Mobeetie to Trinidad, Colorado, where the sheriff not only refused to hold the suspect for him, but threw Poe himself into jail (Poe, *Buckboard Days*, 98).

20. On the night of January 22, 1880, City Marshal Joe Carson confronted four boisterous cowboy revelers who McIntire says were the rustlers he was following, and soon gunfire erupted in the Close and Patterson dancehall in East Las Vegas. Before it was over an estimated forty shots had been fired. Carson lay dead, struck by nine bullets, and William Randall, one of the cowboys, also was killed. James West, another of the cowboys, writhed on the floor, a bullet through his middle. Mysterious Dave Mather, now assistant town marshal in Las Vegas, had been in the center of the action, his six-gun blazing (Howard Bryan, *Wildest of the Wild West*, 130–131).

21. Tom Henry and John Dorsey, the other members of the troublemaking quartet, stole two horses and galloped out of town. Henry had a bullet through the calf of a leg; Dorsey had escaped unharmed (ibid.).

22. Henry and Dorsey were not captured until February 6, two weeks later. A posse that included Dave Rudabaugh, John Joshua Webb, William L. Goodlet, Bill Combs, Lee Smith, and a man named Muldoon surrounded a farmhouse near Mora, thirty miles to the north, and accepted the surrender of the fugitives after giving assurances that they would be protected from mob violence in Las Vegas (ibid., 132–133).

23. Grant did not visit Las Vegas at this time. He and his wife stopped there the following July while conducting a tour of the country after the completion of his term as president (Miguel A. Otero, *My Life on the Frontier*, 209).

24. On February 7, 1880, Dorsey and West were strung up on a windmill that stood in the center of the plaza (Bryan, *The Wildest of the Wild West*, 134).

Chapter 10. Life in New Mexico

1. "Mysterious Dave" Mather was appointed to succeed the late Joe Carson as city marshal, but resigned after only a few weeks because of low pay. Reported the *Las Vegas Daily Optic* of March 3, 1880: "Dave Mather has

resigned his position as town marshal and J. J. Webb will no longer serve as an officer, owing to the inadequacy of the pay received for performing the duties assigned to them. An officer who does his duty should be paid promptly and well. No man can afford to work for nothing, particularly at the risk of his life." Policemen's wages in Las Vegas were far from the $12 per day quoted by McIntire. After the resignation of Mather and Webb, a meeting of concerned citizens was held to deal with the police problem, and it was proposed to hire six new officers at a salary of $30 per month, payable in county scrip *(Las Vegas Daily Optic,* March 5, 1880).

McIntire was not even in Las Vegas during this period. He returned to Mobeetie and remained until at least July, as he is reported in attendance as deputy sheriff that month in the records of proceedings of the district court of Wheeler County (Porter, *Memory Cups,* 97). McIntire does not exaggerate the toughness of Las Vegas, however. J. H. Koogler, editor of the *Las Vegas Gazette,* coined a phrase which became popular in all the wild towns of the West with the remark, "Well, I wonder who they had for breakfast this morning." There were twenty-nine murders recorded in a thirty-day period (Milton W. Callon, *Las Vegas, New Mexico: The Town That Wouldn't Gamble,* 108).

2. On July 4, 1879, Las Vegas celebrated the arrival of the steel rails of the Atchison, Topeka, and Santa Fe Railroad. To distinguish it from "Old Town," the new town erected near the tracks was called "East Las Vegas," and this was the scene of all the action and the source of a law and order problem. After McIntire returned to Las Vegas, sometime in the latter half of 1880, he accepted appointment as a policeman in Old Town. The *Daily Optic* reported on February 9, 1881, that the previous night "was a howling wilderness of flying lead," with bullets creasing the air and sharp reports disturbing the sleep of honest citizens. "We must have a police force on the east side and the braver the men the better the force and fewer the deviltries," the paper's editor said, adding that "Officer McIntyre will accept a position on the police force on this side if he can have a good assistant and if the citizens guarantee living wages to two men. He thinks Frank Stewart is about the chap to hold the position with him and the *Optic* is of the opinion that these two fellows are capable of holding down the town when it comes to rackets with killers."

But on February 11 a committee appointed to recommend a way to raise funds for adequate police protection reported it had no solution and no action was taken (Callon, *Las Vegas,* 109). McIntire's chosen assistant, Frank Stewart, had been a member of the Pat Garrett posse who captured Billy the Kid, Dave Rudabaugh, and other fugitives and brought them to Las Vegas a few months before. Jim East, who was also a member of the posse, later said that Garrett held Stewart in low regard as a lawman: "Garrett knew [Stewart] wouldn't fight and when we slipped up on the house [containing the outlaws] he detailed him to hold the horses. But he was a loose sort of fellow, and made quite a hero of himself when the reporters swarmed down on us at Las Vegas" (Jim East, interviewed by J. Evetts Haley, Douglas, Arizona, September 27, 1927).

3. In early March, 1880, East Las Vegas Justice of the Peace and Acting Coroner Hyman G. Neill, also known as "Hoodoo Brown," slipped out of town "between days," taking with him a bankroll lifted from a murdered citizen. Having earlier arrived in Las Vegas with the railroad, Neill soon established himself as the leader of what became known as the "Dodge City Gang" because so many of its members had formerly been active in that Kansas cowtown. As the first justice of the peace in East Las Vegas, he oversaw and administered the work of the bunco men, tinhorn gamblers, whoremongers, and thugs who descended on the town. Col. William Steele, Jr., a man "ripe in years and experience," was named to replace him. Steele was said to have served four years as sheriff and a year as auditor of Wabash County, Indiana. At this time W. G. Ward was appointed city marshal and B. F. Johnson, assistant (Bryan, *Wildest of the Wild West*, 147–153; *Las Vegas Daily Optic*, March 10, 1880).

4. McIntire suggests that Steele's malfeasance started right in where Neill's ended, using the police as enforcers in an extortion racket. Considering the meager pay given the officers, it is not surprising that they would be tempted to participate in this corruption.

5. On December 26, 1880, Lincoln County Sheriff-elect Pat Garrett arrived in Las Vegas leading a posse that included Barney Mason, Lee Hall, Frank Stewart, Jim East, and "Poker Tom" Emory. They had in tow Dave Rudabaugh, Billy the Kid Bonney, Tom Pickett, and Billie Wilson, all of whom had been captured at Stinking Springs (Leon Metz, *Pat Garrett: The Story of a Western Lawman*, 81; Bryan, *Wildest of the Wild West*, 173). "Tom Fowler" is not mentioned in any accounts.

6. McIntire somewhat garbled this information. On April 2, 1880, Dave Rudabaugh and a man named John Llewellyn, alias "Little Allen," attempted to free their pal, John Joshua Webb, who was in the Las Vegas jail on a murder charge. The unsuccessful effort ended when Webb unaccountably refused to flee and Allen shot and killed the jailor, Antonio Lino Valdez. Seven months later, on November 10, 1880, Webb and several other prisoners escaped from the jail. He was recaptured sixteen days later by Garrett's posse while they searched for the Rudabaugh–Billy the Kid gang (Bryan, *Wildest of the Wild West*, 162–170).

7. Sheriff Desiderio Romero was responding to local Hispanics' condemnation of Rudabaugh because of the part he had played in the killing of jailor Valdez.

8. "As the train was ready to leave the depot," reported the *Las Vegas Daily Optic*, "an unsuccessful attempt was made by Sheriff [Desiderio] Romero

to secure Radabaugh [*sic*] and return him to the county jail. The engineer of the outgoing train was covered by guns, and ordered not to move his engine" (quoted in Bryan, *Wildest of the West*, 178). Jim East, one of Garrett's posse-men, confirmed McIntire's involvement in this affair in a 1927 interview with historian J. Evetts Haley: "Three Americans, heavily armed, came down from new town. [They] were friends of ours, Jim McIntire, George Close, and a man named George Poindexter, a gambler there. McIntire had been in the Texas rangers. They came in behind the mob, and had it between us and them, and that made the mob take notice" (Jim East, interview with Haley, September 27, 1927).

9. The officer who took over the throttle of the engine was identified by the *Las Vegas Gazette* as "Detective J. F. Morley, a special officer of the post office department" (December 28, 1880). This was confirmed by Jim East, who said that Morley, who hailed from Klamath Falls, Oregon, had been a railroad engineer. "The mob had the engineer and fireman with guns on them and wouldn't let the train pull out," said East. "Morley said to Garrett, 'I've been an engineer, and if you'll let me, I'll slip down there through the mob, get in the cab, pull the throttle open, and we'll get out of here.' Garrett said, 'Good, go to it.' . . . Morley sneaked into the cab and jerked the throttle open. He was a little excited, I guess, and jerked it wide open, and the wheels spun around, but it took hold and by the time we got to the end of the walk it seemed like it was going a mile a minute, and the Mexicans stood there with their mouths open" (East, interview with Haley, September 27, 1927).

10. "As the train rolled out," said the *Las Vegas Gazette*, "[Billy the Kid] lifted his hat and invited us to call and see him in Santa Fe, calling out *adios*" (December 28, 1880).

11. The killing of the "piker," or in today's slang, "snitch," described by McIntire was undoubtedly the murder of Nelson W. Starbird in the early hours of April 8, 1880. Starbird was a hack driver who operated between the Old and the New Town. The "well-known sporting man" who killed him may have been gambler George Poindexter, who would side with McIntire and his partner George Close in the confrontation with the mob at the depot the following De-cember. The hack, with Starbird's body inside, was driven to town by Poindex-ter. There the gambler started the story that it was he, Poindexter, who had been the intended target of unseen assassins in the willows, and that Starbird had been killed by mistake (Otero, *My Life*, 205).

Although McIntire states that after this incident gamblers were not both-ered, he was charged at the August 1881 session of the District Court of San Miguel County, Las Vegas, with "keeping a gaming table," and "breaking Sunday law." He had apparently neglected to pay the customary fines which in effect were licensing fees that authorized public gambling (San Miguel County Criminal Docket, 1881, New Mexico State Archives).

12. At a meeting of concerned citizens in Judge Steele's office on March 23, 1881, Arthur Jilson was named city marshal at East Las Vegas, and H. J. Franklin became his assistant. Funds had been found somewhere, and the officers were to be paid $100 a month (Callon, *Las Vegas*, 109).

13. "Socorro is the one town on the Rio Grande north of El Paso which felt the full shock of gun-rule. . . . It was by turns a Mexican village, a mining town, a railroad town and a cow town" (Harvey Ferguson, *Rio Grande*, 252). McIntire and Close were following the advancing Santa Fe Railroad; its arrival at Socorro turned the sleepy little Spanish-American *pueblo* of 1880 into the fourth largest town in New Mexico by 1885 (Porter A. Stratton, *The Territorial Press of New Mexico, 1834–1912*, 46).

14. A vigilante group calling itself the "Socorro Committee of Safety" was organized in December 1880, after the sensational murder of A. M. Conklin, editor of the *Socorro Sun*, by Hispanic brothers named Baca. Antonio Baca was arrested and shot dead in his cell. Onofrio Baca escaped to Texas but was captured by Texas Ranger Jim Gillett and returned to Socorro. The vigilantes stormed the jail, took Baca out, and hanged him (F. Stanley, *Desperadoes of New Mexico*, 221–236; James B. Gillett, *Six Years with the Texas Rangers*, 211–222). McIntire's assertion that the vigilantes hanged "a man every day" is an extreme exaggeration. Study of the 1881–1884 period, when the organization was active, has documented only six vigilante hangings (Jacqueline Dorgan Meketa to RKD, January 11, 1990).

15. During this period in Socorro there was an orgy of "plundering, robbing, hi-jacking, [and] stage-coach hold-ups" by vigilantes or those claiming to be vigilantes. "They exacted a pretty penny of saloon keepers, dance hall girls, and gamblers if they didn't want their places of business destroyed" (Stanley, *Desperadoes*, 230).

16. This was apparently an Hispanic gambler named Juan Alari who was lynched by the vigilantes after being accused of molesting a nine-year-old girl (Meketa to RKD, January 11, 1990). Hispanics at Socorro called the vigilante group *"Los Colgadores,"* or "The Hangers." Around the territory they were known as "The Socorro Stranglers" (Jacqueline D. Meketa, "The Socorro Stranglers," *True West* 34 [September 1987]: 23).

17. The "shooting up" of Socorro by the two men and the driving of the vigilantes from the streets is unlikely. McIntire and Close undoubtedly belonged to the organization, as "from all accounts, every Anglo man in Socorro was a member of the vigilantes (whether they wanted to be or not) including the town's doctor, ministers, lawyers, etc." (Meketa to RKD, January 11, 1990).

18. Here McIntire again reveals his difficulty with numbers. Lake Valley, a new silver camp in the Black Range, lay more than one hundred miles south-southwest of Socorro. A visitor to the new town in November 1882, two months after its founding, paid two dollars to take the fourteen-mile stagecoach trip from Nutt Station, the closest point on the railroad; he reported that the "entire road was filled with loaded wagons, all on their way to this new eldorado." He found that "water is conspicuous by its absence and the dust is terrible," but "the town is flourishing and the town lots command a handsome figure." Hotel accommodations were scarce, but he secured a room for $1.50: "The family washstand was a feature of this hostelry. It consisted of a cracker box and a tin basin in the back yard, a chunk of rosin soap, a filthy towel and a barrel of water with a tin dipper." A note attached to the barrel cautioned against the waste of water *(Las Vegas Daily Optic,* November 15, 1882). By the end of the year Lake Valley would boast of five hundred residents; at its peak several years later it would have a population of about a thousand (Stanley, *Lake Valley,* 9–13).

19. The Lake Valley visitor reported in November: "Jim McIntyre, formerly an officer on the Las Vegas police force, is marshal here and draws a salary of three hundred dollars a month. He holds the reins with a steady hand" *(Las Vegas Daily Optic,* November 15, 1882). McIntire's $300-a-month salary was "an enormous sum for the day. Presumably he earned it" (Ralph Looney, *Haunted Highways: The Ghost Towns of New Mexico,* 173).

While remarking on McIntire's "steady hand," the Lake Valley visitor noted that "the town has two marshals" *(Las Vegas Daily Optic,* November 15, 1882). The second was T. I. "Jim" Courtright, whom McIntire had known at Mobeetie at the time of the ill-conceived Marshal Norton raid. Courtright had been hired, according to Eugene Cunningham, through the intervention of Albert J. Fountain, who held financial interests in Lake Valley and doubts, apparently, concerning McIntire. Fountain approached former Texas Ranger James B. Gillett and offered him the Lake Valley job at double his current pay as police chief at El Paso. Gillett declined but reportedly suggested Jim Courtright for the job. According to Cunningham, and repeated by F. Stanley, Courtright's biographer, Fountain then hired Courtright (Cunningham, *Triggernometry,* 205–206; Stanley, *Jim Courtright,* 91.) It is curious that T. C. Richardson, another writer who knew Gillett well, quoted the former lawman as saying that he had recommended Jim McIntire for the marshal's job at Lake Valley (T. C. Richardson, "A Quart of Bullets," *Frontier Times* 14 [August 1937]: 494). Perhaps he recommended both of them. McIntire makes no mention of Courtright as an officer of the town, but if Fountain did arrange to bring in Courtright with the intent of replacing McIntire in the lucrative position, it would do much to explain the bitter animosity McIntire expresses for Fountain.

While serving as Lake Valley marshal, Courtright reportedly "laid two ore thieves to rest. . . . during a running gun battle [and] killed three other men with his deadly guns" (Looney, *Haunted Highways,* 173; Stanley, *Lake Valley,* 10).

20. This, evidently, was not the Tom Wilson of Palo Pinto County, Texas, who had fought Indians with McIntire back in 1874. A close friend and supporter of both McIntire and Jim Courtright, this Tom Wilson was reportedly robbed and railroaded out of town by enemies of the two Texas gunmen after their escape from murder charges in the later American Valley affair (Rasch, "Murder in American Valley," 6).

21. Staked Plains.

22. Born in New York in 1838, Albert Jennings Fountain was at times military officer, newspaperman, lawyer, customs official, and politician. In 1883, as a major of territorial militia, he began a campaign to clean out the gangs of rustlers who had been preying on the herds of cattlemen in southern New Mexico. Most of those he enlisted were Hispanics; Anglos opposed to the policies of Fountain and his boss, Governor Lionel Sheldon, derisively referred to the force as "the Greaser Militia" (A. M. Gibson, *The Life and Death of Colonel Albert Jennings Fountain,* 112–120).

23. Undercover investigation by militia officers disguised as cowboys convinced Fountain that the major rustler gang, led by John Kinney, was headquartered at Lake Valley. Between thirty and forty outlaws and gunmen, many of them fugitives from Texas, were reported to have taken refuge in the vicinity. In the early hours of March 22, 1883, Fountain raided a ranch near Lake Valley and arrested six suspects, including Butch Hill, John Watts, and Jimmie Hughes. The militiamen started for Hillsboro with their prisoners. At a stop for breakfast shortly after dawn, Hill, Watts, and Hughes made a break for freedom. Rifle fire brought down all three and the bodies were left where they fell. Another militia company mounted a raid at Kingston, where John Shannon, for whom warrants were held, was killed as he attempted escape across rooftops (ibid., 123). McIntire apparently confused the two incidents in his narrative; the three bodies he helped bury near Lake Valley were those of Hill, Watts, and Hughes.

"John Watts, the rustler killed at Lake Valley last week, was a rustler from pure love of the business, and not from poverty or necessity," reported *The Lone Star,* an El Paso newpaper. "He recently sold a mine from which he realized something like $20,000 and yet, with this money in his pocket, he deliberately 'jined the gang' and chose the life of a thief and outlaw, rather than that of an honest man" (March 28, 1883).

24. Jack Sheddon, a hard-drinking prospector, had made a big strike at Leadville, Colorado, and then had squandered half a million dollars. On August

6, 1882, he discovered a rich outcropping in New Mexico's Black Range, triggering a rush which culminated in the development of Kingston (Looney, *Haunted Highways*, 161; F. Stanley, *The Kingston Story*, 5).

25. Lionel Allen Sheldon was born in Worcester, New York, in 1828 and was raised in Ohio. After graduation from law school he was admitted to the bar in Ohio and served as a probate judge in Loraine County. During the Civil War he was brigadier general of Ohio Volunteers. Strong partisan activity in the Republican Party and support of James Garfield resulted in his appointment as governor of New Mexico Territory in 1881, a position he held until 1885. He died in California in 1917 (Keleher, *Violence in Lincoln County*, 367–368).

26. An acclaimed hero of the Civil War, General John Alexander Logan (1826–1886) served two terms in the United States Senate representing Illinois. He arrived in Albuquerque on May 5, 1883, leading an entourage that included Henry M. Atkinson, Surveyor-General of New Mexico, and United States Marshal A. L. Morrison. Logan reportedly was interested in investment in the American Valley cattle ranch of John P. Casey and William C. Moore and came to New Mexico to have a look at the property (Rasch, "Murder in American Valley," 2). General Logan would escape implication in the notorious murder case about to explode and in 1884 would be a candidate for presidential nomination on the Republican ticket; eventually he would be named running mate to James G. Blaine in his unsuccessful bid for the White House that year.

27. Born in Illinois in 1845, Courtright served under General Logan in the Civil War, and later scouted for the army in Texas, Arizona, and New Mexico. He subsequently held law enforcement posts as Fort Worth city marshal and deputy U.S. marshal. In 1882 he renewed his acquaintance with McIntire and served with him in the office of town marshal at Lake Valley, where the two also reportedly hired out their guns as ore guards for the Sierra Mining Company. Courtright was highly regarded by General Logan, and it was undoubtedly this association that resulted in the employment of both Courtright and McIntire on the expedition to American Valley (Stanley, *Jim Courtright*, 1–98).

28. On May sixteenth and seventeenth most of the Logan party arrived back in Albuquerque with a number of prisoners charged with various offenses. One of these was John H. Woods, a reputed rustler, who would play an important role in events to follow (Rasch, "Murder in American Valley," 3).

29. A week after the Logan party left the city, word reached Albuquerque of the brutal murder of Robert Elsinger and Alexis Grossetete, partners in the Gieto Ranch, a small cattle-raising operation in the American Valley. Other ranchmen in the district charged that "a large cattle corporation," trying to secure all water rights in the valley, had plotted the killings. It was rumored that

"an eastern syndicate" had offered $600,000 for the valley, with the stipulation that Elsinger and Grossetete be eliminated. The grand jury, in session in Albuquerque, heard testimony from John Woods charging John P. Casey, his brother James, W. C. Moore, Mueller W. Scott, Jim Courtright, and Jim McIntire with the murders. Woods' story was supported by the testimony of Daniel H. McAllister, recently fired Casey ranch manager, who was himself facing charges on eight counts of cattle theft and brand altering. While this was taking place, John P. Casey, Courtright, and McIntire met with Governor Sheldon in Santa Fe to explain their side of the controversy. Sheldon publicly voiced his belief in John Casey's innocence, while significantly avoiding the question of Courtright and McIntire's involvement. But on May 25 the grand jury in Albuquerque brought indictments for first-degree murder against five men: Jim Casey, Moore, Scott, Courtright, and McIntire. Casey and Scott were quickly arrested and jailed; Moore, Courtright, and McIntire had left town and were considered fugitives (Rasch, "Murder in American Valley," 3; Howard Bryan, "Off the Beaten Path," *Albuquerque Tribune*, February 16, 1959; Victor Westphall, "The American Valley Murders," *Ayer y Hoy en Taos* [Fall 1989]: 3–8).

    30. Both McIntire and Jim Courtright held appointments as deputy U.S. marshals. McIntire also held a commission as deputy sheriff of Dona Ana County (Rasch, "Murder in American Valley," 3; Larry D. Ball, *The United States Marshals of New Mexico and Arizona Territories, 1846–1912*, 150).

    31. This is McIntire's first mention of a wife, of whom nothing is known other than that her first name was "Kittie" *(Woodward News*, June 3, 1898). When and where they were married is undetermined.

    32. On the pretext that he was wanted as a witness in the case, Courtright was taken into custody at Lake Valley by Socorro County Sheriff Pete Simpson and William Abbott of the Rocky Mountain Detective Agency. The officers left him in the charge of a deputy sheriff while they proceeded to Kingston after McIntire. But the stage which had taken the lawmen to Lake Valley also brought copies of the May 25 issue of the *Albuquerque Daily Democrat*, which noted the indictment of Courtright and McIntire for murder. Alerted, Courtright contacted McIntire and arranged the escape (Rasch, "Murder in American Valley," 3; Bryan, "Off the Beaten Path," *Albuquerque Tribune*, February 16, 1959).

    33. Lt. Eugene Van Patton commanded Company A of the Second Cavalry Battalion under Fountain (Gibson, *Fountain*, 112).

    34. Juárez, Mexico.

    35. On October 29, 1883, Governor Sheldon approved the issuance of rewards for the apprehension of W. C. Moore, Courtright, and McIntire in the amount of $500 each on two counts of murder (Territory of New Mexico, Governor's Records, 1881–1885, New Mexico State Records Center and Archives,

Santa Fe). Strangely, McIntire makes no mention of W. C. Moore in his narrative, perhaps because Moore had been a lieutenant in the hated "Greaser Militia."

36. No article signed by McIntire has been found in the surviving territorial press files, but editorials severely critical of Fountain and his militia, echoing McIntire's charges, did appear and probably derived from unsigned letters that he sent. Typical was an item entitled "Overstepping Their Authority" in the *Silver City Enterprise* of April 6, 1883:

Territorial militia under command of Major Fountain . . . arrested John Watts and William Dillard [Butch Hill], two alleged rustlers, at Lake Valley. . . . Under a squad of Mexican militia [they] were riddled with bullets, and after being shot down were kicked in the head and face. They were then taken a short distance from the road and partly covered with dirt. The . . . militia . . . claim that the prisoners made an attempt to escape. John Shannon, [well known] in Southern New Mexico, was also arrested and . . . riddled with bullets under the same pretense. . . . His body was left where it fell, until found by the citizens. Shannon has been in this section of the country for twelve years, and has always been known as a peaceable, honorable and hard working man. . . . It is thought by the people [of Lake Valley] that the killing was altogether unnecessary. Even if it were necessary, there is no excuse for the militia to leave the bodies of their victims lying where they fell, without burial. This is barbarious, and it would be far better to do away with the militia altogether than to have citizens murdered under the cloak of their authority. . . . Major Fountain . . . is responsible for the action of his company, and a great deal of hostile feeling is expressed against him at Lake Valley.

In his official report, Fountain wrote: "I ordered that the bodies be covered with loose earth in order to prevent them from being disturbed by coyotes until they could be taken to their friends for decent interment and telephoned Lake Valley the fact of their death with request that their bodies be sent for" (quoted in Stanley, *Jim Courtright,* 95).

37. "The friend in Fort Worth was A. N. Woody, who had served with Courtright on the police force and who had rented his home to the Courtrights when they moved to Fort Worth" (ibid., 143). An El Paso newspaper noted the arrival at Fort Worth of the celebrated fugitives: "Courtright and McIntyre, who were implicated in the murder of Grossette in the American Valley, N.M. and who escaped from the officers at Lake Valley, passing through this city in their flight, are now in Fort Worth. They have been secreted by their friends, who have intimated that any officer who tries to arrest them will be killed" *(The Lone Star,* June 30, 1883).

38. The riverboat *Will Kyle* (not *William Kiled)* was built at Cincinnati in 1879 for the Cincinnati-to-New-Orleans trade. It was a large vessel, 260 feet long, with 33 staterooms of uniform 8-by-8-feet size (Frederick Way, Jr., "Way's Directory of Western Rivers Packets," 314).

39. The *Will Kyle* struck a log at Australia, Mississippi, and sank on November 15, 1883 (ibid., 315).

40. Haws are the fruit of the hawthorn and pawpaws are the berries of the bush of the same name.

41. This was a boat of the "Diamond Jo Line," headed by "Diamond Jo" Reynolds (William. F. Peterson, *Steamboating on the Upper Mississippi, the Water Way to Iowa,* 549).

42. There were reports that McIntire and Courtright spent some of this time together as fugitives in the Dakotas (Rasch, "Murder in American Valley," 7), but McIntire makes no mention of it.

Chapter 11. Captured by the Rangers

1. In 1884 Augustus J. "Gus" Newby constructed a two-story brick building on the corner of Seventh and Ohio streets in Wichita Falls. He moved into the top floor and outfitted the lower level as a saloon and gambling house. A white elephant painted on the outside wall of the upper story gave the saloon its name (Louise Kelly, *Wichita County Beginnings,* 253).

2. On September 27, 1884, C. C. McComas, district attorney at Albuquerque, asked Governor Sheldon to issue requisitions to the governor of Texas for W. C. Moore, Courtright, and McIntire. McComas asked that Sheldon act at the "earliest possible convenience," as "the thing is now ripe here for execution." Harry Richmond, chief of police at Albuquerque, would go for the fugitives, and the requisition was to be "so drawn as to enable Richmond to act in person or to designate any party or parties to act for him in case of necessity." It was common knowledge that Courtright and McIntire were in Texas, but McComas asked that Moore be included in the requisition "as Richmond thinks he has got reliable information of his whereabouts in Texas" (Territory of New Mexico, Governor's Records, 1881–1885, New Mexico State Records Center and Archives, Santa Fe).

On October 16 Richmond arrived at the Texas Ranger camp near Wichita Falls. Two days later Rangers under the command of Capt. G. H. Schmitt arrested McIntire at Wichita Falls. Schmitt timed the arrest to coincide with the apprehension of Courtright in Fort Worth by another Ranger detail *(Dallas Weekly Herald,* October 23, 1884; "Statement of Facts in Courtright and McIntire case," submitted to Adjutant General W. H. King by Capt. George H. Schmitt, commanding Company C, Frontier Battalion, on October 28, 1884, A. G. F).

3. The newspaper reports from Fort Worth indicated that McIntire did not exaggerate the ferment engendered by Courtright's arrest, although the reports do not confirm his version of the ruse employed to accomplish it. "The city [of Fort Worth] is intensely excited tonight over the probable kidnapping of Jim Courtright by seven Rangers," said the *Dallas Weekly Herald:* "Courtright

was last seen at 11 o'clock this morning [October 18] when in company with [Tarrant County-Sheriff] Jim Maddox he went to the depot with the Rangers . . . who asked Courtright to aid them in making an important arrest on some train coming in. Maddox, having some business up town left Courtright, who never suspected bad faith at the hands of the Texas troops" (October 23, 1884). Courtright was held in a hotel room near the depot. "The news spread all over town like a flash," recalled an old Fort Worth resident. "In ten minutes you couldn't push a needle between the crowd that gathered about the place. Every kid three feet high had a gun on and said they would like to see them take Jim Courtright away from here" (Amos Melton in the *Dallas News*, June 9, 1929, quoted in William R. Cox, *Luke Short and His Era*, 154–155). Ranger Lieutenant Grimes, who made the arrest, reported to Captain Schmitt that "at least one thousand or fifteen hundred" converged on the hotel demanding the release of Courtright (Schmitt, "Statement," A. G. F.).

4. Courtright's biographer says that the guns were provided by A. N. Woody and hidden by a waitress named Caroline Brown, who "was particularly grateful to Courtright who had helped her on occasion when over amorous gentlemen gave her a rough time" (Stanley, *Jim Courtright*, 152–153).

5. McIntire does not explain how he could have arranged for the horses while he was under arrest in another town.

6. Guarded by four Rangers and ten deputy sheriffs, McIntire arrived on the Fort Worth and Denver train at seven o'clock. Heavily ironed, he was taken to jail. Reported the Dallas paper: "Shortly after Judge Hood's writ of habeas corpus was served on Captain Schmitt, of the Rangers, but as before he refused to turn the prisoner over to the sheriff. . . . It is now rumored that a mob has determined to release McIntyre and people are rushing toward the jail . . . " *(Dallas Weekly Herald,* October 23, 1884).

There was no forcible rescue, but unquestionably McIntire had the sympathy of many in Fort Worth. At least one local aspirant for higher public office attempted to make political capital from the situation: "United States District Attorney J. C. Bigger, Republican candidate for Congress, . . . assured McIntyre that he would do all he could to have the governor revoke the requisition. . . . Hundreds of Democrats say that they will vote for Republican or Independent candidates for governor. . . . A Texan who would deliberately surrender two Americans, to be slaughtered by a mob is unworthy of their support . . ." *(Dallas Weekly Herald,* October 23, 1884).

Dispatches to the *San Antonio Daily Express* from Fort Worth reflected the great emotion gripping the town. It was reported on October 24 that "Mrs. MacIntyre" [*sic*] was in Fort Worth, saying that if the authorities returned her husband to New Mexico she would accompany him, but would "kill him with her own hand" before "seeing him mobbed." Some people believed "the government," evidently the federal authorities, "should take some steps" to insure that McIntire was given "a fair trial by his peers and not before twelve Mexicans." It was reported that "a prominent Washington lawyer" had offered to defend Courtright and McIntire at no charge *(San Antonio Daily Express,* October 24, 1884). When a hearing was held on a writ of habeas corpus the courtroom was crowded and looked like "a military tribunal": eight Rangers took stations around the room "with rifles in hand as if looking for a fight." McIntire's friends said they would "obtain aid from the national army" if he were forced to go back" (ibid., October 25, 1884).

7. The jailer was identified as A. J. Lackey by the *Dallas Weekly Herald* of December 13, 1884.

8. Again McIntire is woefully inaccurate on a date. In July he had not yet been arrested. The escape took place on December 11, 1884, two months after his incarceration in the Decatur jail. According to the newspaper account four other prisoners escaped with McIntire and Henry Tickle, a horsethief (ibid.).

9. A Dallas reporter claimed to have information that on December 12, the night after McIntire's escape, he and Courtright met in Fort Worth, took a drink at one of the principal saloons, consulted with several devoted friends, and hurriedly left after each purchased a quart of whiskey. "Both desperadoes were armed to the teeth"; officers believed they had "a hiding place in some of the Trinity thickets of Tarrant County" *(San Antonio Daily Express,* December 13, 1884).

10. "The White Elephant" was a popular name for Texas saloons in the 1880s. McIntire gambled in resorts of that name in both Wichita Falls and Denison. Conflict over the gambling interests in Fort Worth's White Elephant Saloon led to Courtright's death outside the establishment on February 8, 1887. Courtright, who owned the T. I. C. Detective Agency in town, tried to pressure gambler Luke Short into paying for "protection," which Short considered a form of extortion. The dispute led to a gunfight in which Courtright was killed at the age of forty-two.

Chapter 12. Again in the Toils

1. It has often been asserted that after his escape McIntire went to South America, where he joined Jim Courtright (Cunningham, *Triggernometry,* 212; Hunter and Rose, *The Album of Gunfighters,* 158). This story evidently had its origin in rumors that circulated after the escapes of Courtright and McIntire in 1884. According to one version of this tale the two fugitives had gone to Guatemala and led a force of one hundred men fighting for President Justo Barrios *(New Orleans Times-Democrat,* April 21, 1885; *New Orleans Daily Picayune,*

April 23, 1885). F. Stanley, Courtright's biographer, rejects these reports, stating flatly: "Courtright was never in South America." He suggests that friends of the fugitives spread the stories to confuse the authorities (Stanley, *Jim Courtright,* 162–163). McIntire apparently did intend to leave the country, headed for Central America, but was arrested before his departure.

2. On the afternoon of April 20, 1885, New Orleans authorities, acting on information received from informants, arrested McIntire in the City Hotel. Police Capt. Thomas Reynolds and Detectives T. J. Boasso, Tony Pecora, and Dick Kerwin grabbed him in a water closet. Captain Reynolds was described as "physically almost a giant," and McIntire may have found him big enough for two men, accounting for his statement that there were five arresting officers. The fugitive's "desperate character and skill with firearms was well known," and the policemen took no chances, grabbing McIntire by all four limbs and rushing him to a carriage outside. He denied that he was Jim McIntire and initially refused to give a name, but he had registered under the name "C. T. Rogers" at the City Hotel. Upon arrival at the Central Station, he was booked as "C. T. Rogers, alias McIntyre," and charged with being a fugitive from New Mexico. When searched, the prisoner was found to be unarmed, but he carried a large number of newspaper clippings "relative to the escape and probable whereabouts of Courtwright and McIntyre."

Interviewed by a reporter in his cell that night, McIntire maintained that his name was Rogers; he said he was a twenty-seven-year-old cowboy from the Panhandle of Texas, knew nothing of the charges against him, and had never been guilty of any crime. He was described as "tall, beardless, hair thrown back, broad brim black slouch hat, [with a] clear piercing gray eye" *(New Orleans Times-Democrat,* April 21, 1885; *New Orleans Daily Picayune,* April 21, 1885; Rasch, "Murder in American Valley," 6).

Two days later, after obtaining a search warrant, detectives examined McIntire's valise at the City Hotel and found "a handsome silver-plated bone-handled six-shooter pistol"; twenty-five cartridges; three small fine-toothed saws "for cutting iron bars, with handles so made as to be taken apart and used as knives"; a bottle of chloroform; three packs of monte cards; "a gambler's device for marking cards on the back for swindling purposes"; and "a scrapbook containing memorandums of the money he had recently won in different parts of Kentucky, where it seems he has been lately" *(New Orleans Daily Picayune,* April 23, 1885; *New Orleans Times-Democrat,* April 23, 1885).

3. In February 1885, in a widely publicized case, Patrick Ford and John Murphy were convicted and sentenced to death for the murder of Andrew H. Murphy *(New Orleans Times-Democrat,* May 19, 1885).

4. In May 1885, when legal appeals of the condemned men Ford and Murphy received final rejection, New Orleans papers noted that officials at the

Parish Prison were concerned that an escape might be attempted and were taking unusual measures to prevent a breakout *(New Orleans Times-Democrat,* May 19, 1885). The next day, according to the papers, Pat Ford went to the prison captain and revealed the "sensational intentions" of "some sharp and desperate criminals" for an escape attempt. Named as "the master spirit of the enterprise" was "James McIntire, the desperado from New Mexico" (ibid., May 22, 1885).

5. The prisoners were shaken down after Ford's disclosure, and prisoner Pete Burns was "placed in the dungeon and James McIntire confined to his cell" (ibid.). Apparently there had been reports of explosives involved in the plot, as McIntire indicates; the *Daily Picayune* pointed out that search of the grounds uncovered "no gunpowder nor other explosives to be used" (May 22, 1885).

6. Frank Marion Davis (1848–1900), a native of Alabama, the first elected sheriff of Wichita County, was reelected four times, serving from 1882 to 1890. It is not known why McIntire referred to him as a "black sheep" (Kelly, *Wichita County,* 209; Tise, *Texas County Sheriffs,* 541).

7. On April 22, the day after McIntire's arrest, New Orleans Chief of Police Zach Bachemin received a telegram from Governor Sheldon asking him to hold the prisoner and advising that a requisition was en route *(New Orleans Times-Democrat,* April 23, 1885). After the requisition arrived, McIntire was held in the Parish Prison for more than a month while the Louisiana and New Mexico authorities haggled over the responsibility for the cost of returning him for trial. But McIntire's reported involvement in the prison breakout plot "determined the police authorities to hasten his departure from the city," and shortly thereafter the funds were found. Choosing a circuitous route to avoid Fort Worth, on May 30 Chief Bachemin and Detectives T. J. Boasso and C. C. Cain "quietly took their man over the Illinois Central to Kennerville, . . . over the Mississippi Valley to Memphis, thence to Kansas City, from which point they started on June 1 . . . and yesterday arrived at Albuquerque . . ." (ibid., June 4, 1884). "McIntire . . . had so many friends at Fort Worth that the officers brought him to Albuquerque by way of Kansas City for fear his friends might attempt to capture him at Fort Worth" *(Albuquerque Journal,* June 8, 1885). The newspapers reported that McIntire had not been ironed during the journey, but two Albuquerque policemen waiting at the depot snapped handcuffs on him when they took custody. There was no mention of a stop at Santa Fe and an audience with Governor Sheldon (Rasch, "Murder in American Valley," 6; Stanley, *Lake Valley,* 8).

8. Sheriff of Bernalillo County, New Mexico, in 1885 was Santiago Baca (Marc Simmons, *Albuquerque: A Narrative History,* 235).

9. The *Albuquerque Journal* reported that "quite a number of men" called at the jail to see McIntire, but only "a few were admitted. Al Conners

supplied him with cigars and chewing tobacco and Jim Lewis with a cot and blankets, and ordered his meals sent to him from a hotel. . . . The officers all speak highly of him" (June 8, 1885). Perhaps contributing to McIntire's discomfort in this jail was the knowledge that his friend from Texas Ranger days, Milton J. Yarberry, had been jerked into eternity in the courtyard outside only two years before.

10. Bail was originally set at $10,000 (not $100,000) and then reduced to $5,000 (Rasch, "Murder in American Valley," 6). George Lail (not "Laile"), a butcher and mining speculator in Albuquerque, was elected mayor the following year ("Dreesen Files," Albuquerque Public Library).

11. Of course, McIntire was charged with the murder of Grossetete and Elsinger, not for removing the bodies of the outlaws killed by Fountain's militia. McIntire employed lawyers H. B. Ferguson and Thomas Phelan to defend him. Murder charges against James Casey and Mueller Scott had earlier been dropped after two trials resulted in hung juries. When McIntire's case came to trial on October 15, 1885, no witnesses appeared against him and a thoroughly frustrated prosecuting attorney requested a dismissal of charges *(Albuquerque Evening Democrat,* October 15, 1885). Following McIntire's release, Courtright gave himself up to Harry Richmond, but there was no more evidence in this case than in that of McIntire, and the charges were dropped early in 1886. A year later Courtright was shot to death in Fort Worth by Luke Short. Authorities never apprehended W. C. Moore, the third fugitive in the American Valley murder case.

Chapter 13. In a Shooting Scrape

1. Harrold is in eastern Wilbarger County on the Red River, the northern border of Texas. It boomed briefly after the arrival of the Fort Worth and Denver Railroad in 1884.

2. Vernon lay west of Harrold on the Western Cattle Trail.

3. Oldham County, directly west of Wheeler County on the western border of the Panhandle, was organized in 1880, and Tascosa became the county seat. When the Fort Worth and Denver railroad line was built across the county in 1887, many Tascosa businesses were moved two miles to a point across the Canadian River and on the railroad. The population of the two towns in 1890 was 350 (Webb, ed., *Handbook of Texas* 2:708).

4. McIntire is consistent in this error. He refers, of course, to the Staked Plains.

5. The LX Ranch was established in the Texas Panhandle in 1877 by Bostonians David T. Beals and W. H. "Deacon" Bates. W. C. "Outlaw Bill" Moore, later involved with McIntire in the American Valley murder case, was

manager of the LX before moving to New Mexico (Margaret Sheers, "The LX Ranch of Texas," *Panhandle-Plains Historical Review* 6 (1933): 45–57).

6. There is no record of this affair in the county and district court files in Wilbarger County (Jana Kennon (Deputy) to RKD, October 29, 1989). McIntire's name appears in the Criminal Court records for Wheeler County only once during this period. In 1886 he was charged with "disturbing the quietude of the bystanders in a public place." On a plea of guilty, the case was "reconsidered and dismissed" (Porter, *Memory Cups*, 155).

7. Panhandle City enjoyed a boom as the terminus of the Panhandle and Santa Fe Railroad in 1887 and became the seat of Carson County when it was organized in 1888 (Webb, ed., *Handbook of Texas* 2:330). McIntire operated a hotel there, according to Father Stanley (Msgr. Crocchiola to RKD, March 20, 1990).

8. During the building of the Fort Worth and Denver City Railroad across Potter County in 1887, a construction camp composed of buffalo-hide huts and shacks, called "Ragtown," sprang up near a lake that early Mexican cowherds called "Amarillo" because of its yellow-colored banks. The city of Amarillo had not yet developed in the period of which McIntire writes (Webb, ed., *Handbook of Texas* 1:38–39).

9. Washburn was established on JA Ranch property in Armstrong County. In 1887 the town became a junction point where the Fort Worth and Denver road joined a tap line running to Panhandle City and connecting with the Santa Fe (Webb, ed., *Handbook of Texas* 2:864).

10. George Beauregard Berry was an early resident of Canadian, a railroad town in Hemphill County, where he kept a saloon and opera house (Sinise, *George Washington Arrington*, 68). Berry later became a wealthy contractor and developer in Kansas City, Missouri, and served as an alderman *(Kansas City Star*, February 23, 1944).

11. "In this early day, the saloons flourished, each with a gambling hall adjoining. 'Jim McIntire' and 'Smoky Jim,' two famous gamblers, helped to make the town famous" (J. C. Paul, "Early Days in Carson County, Texas" [MS., Research Center, Panhandle-Plains Historical Museum, Canyon, Texas], 3).

12. On September 16, 1893, the lands known as the "Cherokee Outlet" in the northwest corner of Oklahoma were opened up to settlement, and in "one afternoon, eight million acres were added to Oklahoma Territory, its population was increased by 100,000, and a score of populous cities were born. Woodward, Alva, Enid, Medford, Newkirk, Pawnee and Perry became the seats of seven new counties . . ." (Glenn Shirley, *Guardian of the Law: The Life and Times of William Matthew Tilghman*, 211).

13. "When the Territory was opened, it tore Mobeetie all to pieces. . . .

It just about cleaned the town out. Houses were torn down and moved from Mobeetie to Woodward" (J. L. Sieber to J. Evetts Haley, July 17, 1926, quoted in Harris, *Hide Town*, 37). The town of Woodward "became overnight a mass of settlers, soldiers, railroaders, cattlemen, and gun-toting cowboys" (Shirley, *Temple Houston*, 167). Soon there were businesses of all kinds, including two newspapers and twenty-three saloons. McIntire did not lack competition (ibid., 174).

14. The *Woodward News* of March 25, 1898, announced that "Mr. and Mrs. Jim McIntyre have moved to Hot Springs, Arkansas, where they will make their future home." In the 1890s Hot Springs was developing its reputation as the Monte Carlo of the Middle West. It featured a race track and plush resorts offering gambling games of all sorts. But, said a veteran professional, "There was not a club on the square" (Henry Chafetz, *Play the Devil: A History of Gambling in the United States From 1492 to 1955*, 394).

15. McIntire apparently did not go directly to Mountain View but spent some time in Guthrie, Oklahoma Territory, another gambling center. His wife had returned to Woodward from Hot Springs and, as reported in the *Woodward News* of June 3, 1898, "Mrs. Kittie McIntire left Sunday to make her home in Guthrie, where she and her husband, Jim McIntire, will reside."

On the line of the Chicago, Rock Island, and Pacific Railway, Mountain View was in Kiowa County, southwestern Oklahoma Territory.

Chapter 14. Through Heaven and Hell

1. "There was lots of smallpox in this part of the country at that time. The town of Mountain View was almost completely wiped out by it in 1901. They had a place there where they took those having the dreaded disease, who didn't have anyone to care for them" (Clem A. Trotter, interview by Ruby Wolfenberger, January 19, 1938, Indian Pioneer History, 130 vols., Archives Division, Oklahoma Historical Society, Oklahoma City, 103:344).

2. Obviously, the awful thirst of which McIntire was constantly aware, even in his delirium, was a symptom of the very high fever he was suffering. The hands on his shoulders were undoubtedly those of his nurses.

3. There is no record of a "Dr. Aburnett" in Mountain View, but a Dr. W. Abernathy was practicing there and is doubtless the physician McIntire means (Mary Fellows to RKD, January 16, 1990).

Conclusion

1. McIntire has given few examples of his propensity to steal, although from the days when he absconded with the funds earned by the black minstrels

on the Ohio River to his fleecing of a victim in a Panhandle City monte game, he undoubtedly was quick to grab a dishonest buck (or shinplaster) by stealth or trickery. But he never turned to outright outlawry, and his reporting of Long John Mont's offer to join a vast rustler gang evidenced his rejection of a life on the "owl hoot trail."

2. Although McIntire is still careful neither to admit nor deny his guilt in the American Valley murders, here, at least, he drops the fiction that he was wanted for burying the bodies of Fountain's victims. He was not "exonerated," however: he was simply not prosecuted. Cheerfully confessing to the killing and mutilation of Indians, he admits nowhere in the book to the killing of a white man.

3. Robert Green Ingersoll (1833–1899) was a prominent nineteenth-century trial lawyer, lecturer, and author who was best known for his strong, frequently expressed, agnostic views.

Bibliography

Books

Adams, Ramon F. *Burs Under the Saddle: A Second Look at Books and Histories of the West*. Norman: University of Oklahoma Press, 1964.
———. *Six-Guns and Saddle Leather*. Norman: University of Oklahoma Press, 1969.
Ball, Larry D. *The United States Marshals of New Mexico and Arizona Territories, 1846–1912*. Albuquerque: University of New Mexico Press, 1978.
Bartholomew, Ed. *Wyatt Earp: The Untold Story*. Toyahville, Texas: Frontier Book Co., 1963.
Biggers, Don H. *Shackelford County Sketches*. 1908. Albany and Fort Griffin, Texas: Clear Fork Press, 1974.
Black, A. P. "Ott." *The End of the Long Horn Trail*. Selfridge, N. Dak.: Selfridge Journal, n.d. (ca. 1936).
Bryan, Howard. *Wildest of the Wild West*. Santa Fe, N.M.: Clear Light Publishers, 1988.
Burton, Jeff, ed. *Portraits in Gunsmoke*. London: English Westerners Society, 1971.
Callon, Milton W. *Las Vegas, New Mexico: The Town that Wouldn't Gamble*. Las Vegas, N. Mex.: Las Vegas Daily Optic, 1962.
Chafetz, Henry. *Play the Devil: A History of Gambling in the United States From 1492 to 1955*. New York: Clarkson N. Potter, 1960.
Clarke, Mary Whatley. *The Palo Pinto Story*. Fort Worth, Texas: Manney Co., 1956.
Clift, G. Glenn. *History of Maysville and Mason County*. Lexington, Ky.: Transylvania Printing Co., 1936.
Colletta, Lillian, and Leslie Puckett. *Tombstone Inscriptions of Brown County, Ohio*. Denville, N.J.: Lillian Colletta, 1963.
Collins, Richard H. *Collins' Historical Sketches of Kentucky; History of Kentucky*. Vol. 1. Frankfurt, Ky.: Kentucky Historical Society, 1966.
Cox, William R. *Luke Short and His Era*. Garden City, N.Y.: Doubleday and Co., 1961.
Craige, Capt. John Houston. *The Practical Book of American Guns*. Cleveland and New York: World Publishing Co., 1950.
Cunningham, Eugene. *Triggernometry: A Gallery of Gunfighters*. 1934. Caldwell, Idaho: Caxton Printers, 1962.
DeArment, Robert K. *Bat Masterson: The Man and the Legend*. Norman: University of Oklahoma Press, 1979.

Donaldson, Patricia R. *Brown County, Ohio, Marriage Records, 1818–1850.* N.p.: Patricia R. Donaldson, 1986.

Ferguson, Harvey. *Rio Grande.* New York: Alfred A. Knopf, 1940.

Gard, Wayne. *Frontier Justice.* Norman: University of Oklahoma Press, 1949.

———. *Sam Bass.* Boston and New York: Houghton Mifflin Co., 1936.

Garrett, Pat F. *The Authentic Life of Billy, the Kid.* Norman: University of Oklahoma Press, 1954.

Gibson, A. M. *The Life and Death of Colonel Albert Jennings Fountain.* Norman: University of Oklahoma Press, 1965.

Gieck, Jack. *A Photo Album of Ohio's Canal Era, 1825–1913.* Kent, Ohio: Kent State University Press, 1988.

Gillett, James B. *Six Years with the Texas Rangers.* New Haven: Yale University Press, 1925.

Haley, J. Evetts. *Charles Goodnight: Cowman and Plainsman.* Boston and New York: Houghton Mifflin Co., 1936.

———. *Jeff Milton: A Good Man With a Gun.* Norman: University of Oklahoma Press, 1948.

Hamilton, Allen Lee. *Sentinel of the Southern Plains: Fort Richardson and the Northwest Frontier, 1866–1878.* Fort Worth: Texas Christian University Press, 1988.

Harris, Sallie B. *Hide Town in the Texas Panhandle.* Hereford, Texas: Pioneer Book Publishers, 1968.

Haywood, C. Robert. *Trails South: The Wagon-Road Economy in the Dodge City–Panhandle Region.* Norman and London: University of Oklahoma Press, 1986.

Hening, H. B., ed. *George Curry, 1861–1947: An Autobiography.* Albuquerque: University of New Mexico Press, 1958.

History of Brown County, Ohio. Chicago: W. H. Beers and Co., 1883.

Horton, Thomas F. *History of Jack County.* 1932. N.p.: 1975.

Huckabay, Ida Lasater. *Ninety-Four Years in Jack County, 1854–1948.* Waco, Texas: Texian Press, 1974.

Hunter, John Marvin, and Noah H. Rose. *The Album of Gunfighters.* Bandera, Texas: 1951.

Johnson, Barry C., ed. *"Ho, For the Great West!"* London: English Westerners' Society, 1980.

Keleher, William A. *Violence in Lincoln County, 1869–1881.* Albuquerque: University of New Mexico Press, 1957.

Kelly, Louise. *Wichita County Beginnings.* Austin, Texas: Eakin Press, 1982.

Ledbetter, Barbara A. Neal. *Fort Belknap Frontier Saga.* Burnet, Texas: Eakin Press, 1982.

Lloyd, James T. *Lloyd's Steamboat Directory and Disasters on the Western Waters.* Cincinnati, Ohio: J. T. Lloyd Co., 1856.

Looney, Ralph. *Haunted Highways: The Ghost Towns of New Mexico.* New York: Hastings House, Publishers, 1968.

McCarty, John L. *Maverick Town: The Story of Old Tascosa.* Norman: University of Oklahoma Press, 1946.

McKenna, James A. *Black Range Tales.* Glorieta, N. Mex.: Rio Grande Press, 1976.

McLoughlin, Denis. *Wild and Woolly: An Encyclopedia of the Old West.* Garden City, N.Y.: Doubleday and Co., 1975.

Malone, Dumas, ed. *Dictionary of American Biography.* New York: Chas. Scribner's Sons, 1934.

Metz, Leon. *John Selman: Texas Gunfighter.* 1966. Norman: University of Oklahoma Press, 1980.

——. *Pat Garrett: The Story of a Western Lawman.* Norman: University of Oklahoma Press, 1974.

Nye, W. S. *Carbine and Lance: The Story of Old Fort Sill.* Norman: University of Oklahoma Press, 1937.

Otero, Miguel A. *My Life on the Frontier.* New York: Press of the Pioneers, 1935.

Paddock, Capt. B. B. *A Twentieth Century History and Biographical Record of North and West Texas.* Vol. 1. Chicago and New York: Lewis Publishing Co., 1906.

Parker, Morris B. *White Oaks: Life in a New Mexico Gold Camp, 1880–1900.* Tucson: University of Arizona Press, 1971.

Payne, Darwin. *Dallas: An Illustrated History.* Woodland Hills, Calif.: Windsor Publications, 1982.

Peterson, William F. *Steamboating on the Upper Mississippi: The Water Way to Iowa.* Iowa City, Iowa: State Historical Society of Iowa, 1937.

Poe, Sophie. *Buckboard Days.* Caldwell, Idaho: Caxton Printers, 1936.

Porter, Millie Jones. *Memory Cups of Panhandle Pioneers.* Clarenden, Texas: Clarenden Press, 1945.

Rath, Ida Ellen. *The Rath Trail.* Wichita, Kans.: McCormick-Armstrong Co., 1961.

Rathjen, Frederick W. *The Texas Panhandle Frontier.* Austin and London: University of Texas Press, 1975.

Reed, Paula, and Grover Ted Tate. *The Tenderfoot Bandits, Sam Bass and Joel Collins: Their Lives and Hard Times.* Tucson, Ariz.: Westernlore Press, 1988.

Rickards, Colin. *Mysterious Dave Mather.* Santa Fe, N. Mex.: Press of the Territorian, 1968.

Rister, Carl Coke. *Fort Griffin on the Texas Frontier*. Norman: University of Oklahoma Press, 1956.

Rogers, John William. *The Lusty Texans of Dallas*. New York: E. P. Dutton and Co., 1951.

Shirley, Glenn. *Guardian of the Law: The Life and Times of William Matthew Tilghman*. Austin, Texas: Eakin Press, 1988.

———. *Temple Houston: Lawyer With a Gun*. Norman: University of Oklahoma Press, 1980.

Simmons, Marc. *Albuquerque: A Narrative History*. Albuquerque: University of New Mexico Press, 1982.

Sinise, Jerry. *George Washington Arrington: Civil War Spy, Texas Ranger, Sheriff and Rancher*. Burnet, Texas: Eakin Press, 1979.

Siringo, Charles A. *Riata and Spurs*. Boston and New York: Houghton Mifflin Co., 1927.

Sonnichsen, C. L. *I'll Die Before I'll Run: The Story of the Great Feuds of Texas*. 1951. New York: Devin-Adair Co., 1962.

Stanley, F. *Desperadoes of New Mexico*. Denver, Colo.: World Press, 1953.

———. *Jim Courtright: Two Gun Marshal of Fort Worth*. Denver, Colo.: World Press, 1957.

———. *The Kingston (New Mexico) Story*. Pantex, Texas: F. Stanley, 1961.

——— *The Lake Valley (New Mexico) Story*. Pep, Texas: F. Stanley, 1964.

Stratton, Porter A. *The Territorial Press of New Mexico, 1834–1912*. Albuquerque: University of New Mexico Press, 1969.

Thompson, Carl N. *Historical Collections of Brown County, Ohio*. Piqua, Ohio: Hammer Graphics, 1969.

Thrapp, Dan L. *Encyclopedia of Frontier Biography, In Three Volumes*. Glendale, Calif.: Arthur H. Clark Co., 1988.

Tise, Sammy. *Texas County Sheriffs*. Albuquerque, N. Mex.: Oakwood Printing, 1989.

Webb, Walter Prescott. *The Texas Rangers: A Century Of Frontier Defense*. Boston and New York: Houghton Mifflin Co., 1935.

———, ed. *The Handbook of Texas*. Austin: Texas State Historical Association, 1952.

Articles

Carnal, Ed. "Reminiscences of a Texas Ranger." *Frontier Times* 1 (December 1923): 20–24.

Cross, Cora Melton. "Ira Long, Cowboy and Texas Ranger." *Frontier Times* 8 (October 1930): 22–31.

DeArment, R. K. "The Blood-Spattered Trail of Milton J. Yarberry." *Old West* 22 (Fall 1985): 8–14.

————. "The Great Outlaw Confederacy." *True West* 37 (September 1990) 14–19.

Haley, J. Evetts. "Jim East—Trail Hand and Cowboy." *Panhandle-Plain Historical Review 6* (1931): 39–61.

McConnell, H. H. "The Massacre of Henry Warren's Train." *Frontier Times* 2 (May 1925): 16–22.

Meketa, Jacqueline D. "The Socorro Stranglers." *True West* 34 (September 1987): 22–25.

Oswald, James M. "History of Fort Elliott." *Panhandle-Plains Historical Review* 32 (1959) 1–59.

Purdy, R. S. "Fight with Indians at Loving's Ranch." *Frontier Times* 2 (June 1925): 1–2.

Rasch, Philip J. "Murder in American Valley." *English Westerners' Brand Book* 6 (April 1965): 2–7.

Rattenbury, Richard. "Shooting a Stand: Buffalo Rifles on the West Texas Frontier." *Man at Arms* 9 (November-December 1987).

"Record of Engagement With Hostile Indians in Texas 1868–1882." *West Texas Historical Association Yearbook* 9 (1933): 101–118.

Richardson, T. C. "A Quart of Bullets," *Frontier Times* 14 (August 1937): 490–494.

Robertson, Walter M. "The Loss Valley Fight." *Frontier Times* 7 (December 1929): 100–104.

Robinson, Charles M. III. "John Larn." *True West* 36 (October 1989): 21–27.

Sheers, Margaret. "The LX Ranch of Texas." *Panhandle-Plains Historical Review* 6 (1933): 45–57.

Sheffy, L. F., "Old Mobeetie—The Capital of the Panhandle." *West Texas Historical Association Yearbook* 6 (1930): 3–16.

Streeter, Floyd B. "The Millet Cattle Ranch in Baylor County, Texas." *Panhandle-Plains Historical Review* 22 (1949): 65–83.

"Trails Grown Dim." *Frontier Times* 52 (August-September 1978): 1.

Turner, John M. "Indian Fight in Loving County in 1874." *Frontier Times* 30 (1953): 236.

Westphall, Victor. "The American Valley Murders," *Ayer y Hoy en Taos* 9 (Fall 1989): 3–8.

Newspapers

Albuquerque Daily Democrat.
Albuquerque Evening Democrat.

Albuquerque Journal.
Albuquerque Tribune.
Austin American.
Dallas Weekly Herald.
Dodge City Times.
Galveston Daily News.
Kansas City Star.
Las Vegas (N. Mex.) *Gazette.*
Las Vegas (N. Mex.) *Daily Optic.*
Las Vegas (N. Mex.) *Weekly Optic.*
Lone Star, The (El Paso, Texas)
New Orleans Daily Picayune.
New Orleans Times-Democrat.
San Antonio Daily Express.
Silver City Enterprise.
Weatherford Democrat.
Woodward News.

Letters

Crocchiola, Msgr. Stanley, to Robert K. DeArment, March 20, 1990.
Ernst, Robert R. to Robert K. DeArment, September 25, 1989.
Fellows, Mary to Robert K. DeArment, January 16, 1990.
Meketa, Jacqueline Dorgan, to Robert K. DeArment, January 11, 1990.
Morrison, Richard, to Robert K. DeArment, April 6, 1990.

Unpublished Materials

Adjutant-General's Files [A.G.F.] Archives Division, Texas State Library, Austin, Texas.
Burns, Rollie. "Reminiscence of 56 Years." Nita Stewart Haley Memorial Library, Midland, Texas.
"Dreesen Files." Albuquerque Public Library, Albuquerque, N. Mex.
East, James. Interview by J. Evetts Haley, Douglas, Arizona, September 27, 1927. Nita Stewart Haley Memorial Library, Midland, Texas.
Indian Pioneer History. 130 vols. Archives Division, Oklahoma Historical Society, Oklahoma City, Okla.
Lamborn Collection. Kansas State Historical Society, Topeka, Kans.
McIntire, James. Sworn Statement of James McIntire before Moses Wiley, June 30, 1879. Research Center, Panhandle-Plains Historical Museum, Canyon, Texas.

Paul, J. C. "Early Days in Carson County, Texas." Research Center, Pan-handle-Plains Historical Museum, Canyon, Texas.

Perkins, William C. "A History of Wheeler County, Texas." Research Center, Panhandle-Plains Historical Museum, Canyon, Texas.

San Miguel County Criminal Court Docket, 1881. New Mexico State Records Center and Archives, Santa Fe.

Territory of New Mexico, Governor's Records, 1881–1885. New Mexico State Records Center and Archives, Santa Fe.

U.S. Bureau of the Census. Seventh Census of the United States, 1850. Population Schedules. Washington, D.C.: National Archives and Records Service.

————. Eighth Census of the United States, 1860. Population Schedules. Washington, D.C.: National Archives and Records Service.

————. Ninth Census of the United States, 1870. Population Schedules. Washington, D.C.: National Archives and Records Service.

Way, Frederick, Jr. "Way's Directory of Western Rivers Packets." Louisiana Department, Louisiana State Library, Baton Rouge.

Wiley, Moses. Letter to Texas Ranger Major John B. Jones, July 1, 1879. Research Center, Panhandle-Plains Historical Museum, Canyon, Texas.

Index

Abbott, William: 149n
Abernathy, Dr. W.: 112, 158n
Aburnett, Dr.: *see* Abernathy, Dr. W.
Adams, Ramon F.: 8
Adde, Henry: 101
Alari, Juan: 145n
Albany, Texas: 132n
Albuquerque Daily Democrat: 149n
Albuquerque, N. Mex.: 60, 75, 78, 95–97, 130n, 148n, 149n, 151n, 155n, 156n
Allegheny River: 85
Alopas, N. Mex.: 76
Alva, Okla.: 157n
Amarillo, Texas: 100, 157n
American Valley: 4, 5, 147n–150n, 156n, 159n
Anadarko, Okla.: 129n
Armstrong County, Texas: 157n
Atchison, Topeka, and Santa Fe Railroad: 72–74, 102, 137–38n, 142n, 145n
Atkinson, Henry M.: 148n
Austin, Texas: 63–64
Australia, Miss.: 150n
Ay-cufty (Comanche): 55–56, 130n

Baca, Antonio: 145n
Baca, Onofrio: 145n
Baca, Santiago: 155n
Bachemin, Zach: 155n
Bad Lands, New Mexico: 80–81
Bailey, D. W. ("Dave" or "Ed"): 51–54, 128n, 130n
Barrios, Justo: 153n
Bass, Sam: 4, 5, 64, 133n
Bates, W. H. ("Deacon"): 156n
Baton Rouge, La.: 91
Battle of Adobe Walls: 128n
Battle of Mansfield: 129n
Baylor County, Texas: 134n
Beals, David T.: 156n
Belknap, Texas: 72, 74, 118, 120–27
Bernilillo County, N. Mex.: 155n
Berry, George Beauregard: 4, 100–101, 117n, 157n
Big Lost Valley: 19, 20, 49, 56, 124n, 127n

Big Rocky Mountains: 24
Big Sandy River: 119 n
Big Springs, Nebr.: 133 n
Big Tree (Kiowa): 50, 54, 127 n, 129 n
Big Wichita River: 37, 47, 49
Bigger, J. C.: 152 n
Billy the Kid: 4, 70, 72–74, 141 n–144 n
Black Coyote: 55–56, 130 n
Black Crow: 57–58, 130 n
Black Range: 146 n, 148 n
Blackwell, Dr. J. W. H.: 122 n
Blackwell House, Weatherford, Texas: 18, 122 n
Blaine, James G.: 148 n
Boasso, J. T.: 154 n, 155 n
Bonney, William H.: *see* Billy the Kid
Bowie knife: 128 n
Boyd County, Ky.: 119 n
Bracken County, Ky.: 120 n
Brandenburg, Ky.: 119 n
Brazos River: 31, 32, 34, 48, 57, 63, 126 n
Brown, Caroline: 152 n
Brown, George, Jr. and Sr.: 61, 131 n
Brown, "Hoodoo": 143 n
Brown, Jesse: 61, 131 n
Brown County, Ohio: 11, 85, 119 n, 121 n
Brumbelow, N.: *see* Brumlow, Nath
Brumlow, Nath: 123 n
Buckley, Charley: 39–41, 45, 47
Burns, Pete: 155 n
"Butcher Knife Bill" (Mobeetie character): 135 n

Cain, C. C.: 155 n
Cambren, Mr. and Mrs. James B.: 125 n
Campbell, Lt. G. W. (Texas Ranger): 126 n, 131 n, 132 n, 133 n
Canadian, Texas: 8, 157 n
Canadian River: 70, 98, 136 n, 137 n, 139 n, 156 n
Canadian River Cattle Association: 141 n
Carnal, Ed: 128 n
Carson, "Crosseyed Bob": 123 n
Carson, Joe: 71, 74, 141 n
Carson County, Texas: 157 n

Casey, James: 149n, 156n
Casey, John P.: 148n, 149n
Casto, William T.: 15–16, 120n
Catlettsburg, Ky.: 12, 119n
Chapin, Capt.: *see* Casto, William T.
Charleston (Charlestown), W. Va.: 13, 119n
Chase, Frank: 123n
Cherokee Outlet, Okla.: 157n
Chicago, Rock Island and Pacific Railroad: 158n
Chillicothe, Ohio: 15, 120n
Cincinnati, Ohio: 15, 84, 85, 118n, 119n, 120n, 150n
Citizens' Bank of Roswell: 141n
City Hotel, New Orleans, La.: 92, 154n
Civil War: 13, 119n, 122n, 126n, 129n, 134n, 148n
Clark (Belknap merchant): 66–68
Clay County, Texas: 29, 124n
Clear Creek: 20
Clear Fork of the Brazos: 28, 126n
Cleveland, Ohio: 120n
Close, George: 71, 74–75, 144n, 145n
Close and Patterson Dancehall: 71, 74, 141n
Coalburgh, W. Va.: 119n
Coke, Richard: 127n
Colgodores: 145n
Colorado City, Texas: 84
Colt's revolver: 54
Colt's rifle: 120n
Colton, W.Va.: 13
Comanche Indians: 20, 45, 52, 113, 124n, 130n
Combs, Bill: 141n
Cone, John: 50–51, 128n
Conklin, A. M.: 145n
Conners, Al: 155–56n
Cooke County, Texas: 131n
Cooksey, Jim: 132n
Cooper, Buck, Coon, Harry, and Ira: 123n
Copelan, Charles: 122n
Corn, Lee: 50–51, 128n
Corsicana, Texas: 127n
Courtright, Timothy Isaiah ("Jim"): 4, 69–70, 78–84, 86–87, 138n, 146n–156n

Cox Mountains: 49
Creedmore, Long Island, N. Y.: 126n
Creedmore rifle: 43, 47, 126n
Cribbs: *see* Krebs, Ben
Crocchiola, Fr. Stanley: 8, 146n, 152n, 154n, 157n
Cruger, William: 132n
Cunningham, Eugene: 5, 146n
Curtis, J. C. and W. R.: 28, 124n

Dallas, Texas: 16, 64, 69, 121n, 133n, 134n, 138n, 139n, 152n, 153n
Dameron (Damaron?), Shad: 29, 123n, 124n
Damon, Shad: *see* Dameron, Shad
Davidson, Johnny: 97–99
Davis, Gov. Edmund J.: 127n
Davis, Frank Marion: 94, 155n
Deadwood, Dak. Terr.: 133n
Decatur, Texas: 87, 153n
Deming, N.Mex.: 80
Democratic Party: 152n
Denison, Texas: 16, 90–91, 153n
Denny, Jane: 121n
Denny, Lyman ("Cash"): 16–19, 117n, 121n, 123n
Denny, William: 121n
Denton, Texas: 133n
Denver and Rio Grande Railroad: 138n
Deuce of Hearts (a horse): 101
Devil's River: 136n
DeWees, John O.: 134n
"Diamond Jo" Steamboat Line: 85, 151n
Dillard, William: 77, 147n
Dillingham Prairie, Texas: 122n
Dodge City, Kans.: 71, 137n, 140n, 143n
Dodge City Gang: 143n
Dohauson (Kiowa): 128n
Dona Ana County, N.Mex.: 149n
Donely (Donley), John: 135n
Dorsey, John: 71, 141n
Dover, Ky.: 15, 120n
Dubbs, Emanuel: 139n

Earp, Wyatt: 4, 70, 140n

East, Jim: 72; quoted, 142–43 n, 144 n
Eastham, J. C.: 12, 119 n
East Las Vegas, N.Mex.: 141 n, 143 n, 145 n
El Paso, Texas: 8, 80, 83, 145 n, 146 n, 147 n, 150 n
El Paso del Norte (Juárez), Mexico: 83, 97, 149 n
Elizabethtown, N.Mex.: 139 n
Ellison, James F.: 134 n
Elsinger, Robert: 148 n, 149 n, 156 n
Emory, "Poker Tom": 143 n
England, William G.: 131 n
Enid, Okla.: 157 n

Feather Hill (Mobeetie red-light district): 135 n
Ferguson, H. B.: 156 n
Fish Creek Mountains: 63
Flat Top Mountain: 56–57, 127 n
Fleming, Henry: 68–69, 134 n, 135 n, 138 n, 139 n
Flipper, Lt. Henry Ossian (U.S.A.): 4, 69–70, 138 n, 139 n
"Fly Speck" (Mobeetie character): 135 n
Ford, Patrick: 93, 154 n, 155 n
Ford County, Kans.: 137 n
Fort Belknap, Texas: 41–42, 63, 126 n
Fort Davis, Texas: 140 n
Fort Dodge, Kans.: 70, 136 n, 137 n
Fort Elliott, Texas: 69, 70, 117 n, 134 n, 136 n, 137 n, 139 n
Fort Griffin, Texas: 28, 38, 49, 61–64, 68, 124 n, 125 n, 127 n, 131 n, 132 n,
    133 n, 136 n, 137 n, 140 n
Fort Jacksboro: *see* Fort Richardson
Fort Richardson, Texas: 6, 48, 49, 53, 54, 122 n, 126 n, 130 n
Fort Sill, Indian Territory: 54, 57, 127 n, 138 n
Fort Smith, Ark.: 130 n
Fort Sumner, N.Mex.: 141 n
Fort Worth, Texas: 17, 39, 69, 84, 86–87, 90, 95, 121 n, 122 n, 138 n, 148 n,
    150 n–153 n, 155 n, 156 n
Fort Worth and Denver City Railroad: 152 n, 156 n, 157 n
Fountain, Albert Jennings: 4, 7, 77–80, 146 n, 147 n, 149 n, 150 n, 156 n,
    159 n
Fowler, Tom: 72, 143 n
Franklin, H. J.: 145 n
"Frog Mouth Annie" (Mobeetie character): 135 n

Gainesville, Texas: 61, 131n
Gallipolis, Ohio: 13, 119n
Garfield, Pres. James: 148n
Garrett, Pat: 4, 70, 72–73, 141n–144n
Garsiese, Juan: 75
Gieto Ranch: 148n
Gillette, James B.: 145n, 146n
Gilson, Arthur: 74, 145n
Gilson, William C. ("Big Bill"): 36, 38, 63, 125n, 132n
Glass, Knox: 50–52
Glass, W. A. ("Billy"): 50–53, 128n
Goodell, George: 138n
Goodlet, William L.: 141n
Goodnight, Charles: 135n
Graham, Texas: 28, 48, 121n, 124n, 126n
Grant, Pres. Ulysses S.: 71, 141n
Grimes, Lt. (Texas Ranger): 152n
Gross, John: 136n
Grossette, Alexis: 148n, 149n, 150n, 156n
Guatamala: 153n
Guthrie, Okla.: 158n

Haley, J. Evetts: 144n
Hall, Lee: 143n
Hamilton, Lt. G. R. (Texas Ranger): 49, 59, 64, 126n, 133n
"Hangers": 145n
Harrold, Texas: 97–98, 156n
Haverty, Pete: 136n
Heath, John: 21–24, 123n, 124n
Hemphill County, Texas: 157n
Henry, Fred: 78
Henry, Tom: 71, 141n
Henry rifle: 22, 54
Henson, Jack: 23, 123n
Hewey, Virgil: 136n
Hidetown: *see* Mobeetie, Texas
Hill, "Butch": 77, 147n
Hillsboro, N.Mex.: 147n
Hines, Belle: 135n
Hogg, Gov. James S.: 131n
Holliday, J. H. ("Doc"): 138n

Honduras River: 92
Hood, Judge: 152n
Hopkins, Ky.: 122n
Horton, Thomas F.: 122n, 123n, 125n, 129n
Hot Springs, Ark.: 102, 158n
Houston and Texas Central Railroad: 121n
Houston, Sam: 135n
Houston, Temple: 135n
Howard, G. J.: 139n
Huckabay, Ida Lasater, quoted: 129n, 132n
Hughes, Jimmie: 147n
Hunt, W. C. ("Carr"): 29, 124n
Hunter, J. Marvin: 5
Huntsville Penitentiary: 127n, 129n
Huselby, J. W.: 135n

Illinois Central Railroad: 155n
Indian Territory: 49, 69, 124n, 129n, 139n
Ingersoll, Robert Green: 114, 159n
Ioni (Ironeye) Creek: 64, 133n
Ironton, Ohio: 11, 14, 119n
Isa-toho (Comanche): 55–56, 130n

JA Ranch: 157n
Jack County, Texas: 19, 29, 122n, 124n, 129n, 130n, 132n
Jacksboro (Jacksborough), Texas: 19–22, 28, 36, 38, 122n, 124n–127n, 129n, 134n
Jay, Bill: 123n
Jeffers, "Happy Joe": 15–16, 120n
Jilson, Arthur: 74, 145n
Johnson, B. F.: 143n
Johnson, Walter: 69, 138n
Jones, "Feather Stone": 135n
Jones, John: 99–100
Jones, Major John B. (Texas Ranger): 50, 53, 123n, 127n–129n, 130–31n, 133n, 136n, 137n
Junction Resort, Washburn, Texas: 100–101

Kanawha River: 119n
Kansas City, Mo.: 8, 22, 100, 155n, 157n
Keith, Jones: 123n

Kerwin, Dick: 154n
Kingston, N.Mex.: 78–79, 147n, 148n, 149n
Kinney, John: 147n
Kiowa County, Okla.: 158n
Kiowa Indians: 20, 52, 113, 124n, 127n, 128n
Klamath Falls, Ore.: 144n
Koogler, J. H.: 142n
Krebs, Ben: 61, 131n
Kutch, W. C.: 124n, 125n

Lackey, A. J.: 87–89, 153n
Lail, George A.: 95, 156n
Lake, Stuart N.: 140n
Lake Erie: 120n
Lake Valley, N.Mex.: 75–80, 83, 96, 146n–150n
Larn, John: 4, 63, 132n, 133n, 137n
Las Vegas, N.Mex.: 7, 70–74, 140n–144n, 146n
Las Vegas Gazette: 142n; quoted, 144n
Lawrence County, Ohio: 119n
Lawton, Okla.: 58
Leach, Gravis: 139n
Leadville, Colo.: 138n, 147n
Lee, W. M. D.: 125n
Lee and Reynolds Company: 38, 125n
Lemly, Mother: 135n
Lewis, Jim: 156n
Lincoln County, N.Mex.: 72, 137n, 141n, 143n
Little Wichita River: 37
Llewellyn, John ("Little Allen"): 143n
Locke, Newton F.: 4, 65–68, 134n, 135n
Logan, John Alexander: 4, 78, 148n
Lone Wolf (Kiowa): 124n, 128n
Long, Lt. Ira (Texas Ranger): 54–55, 129, 130n
Long, Johnny: *see* Larn, John
Longhurst, Harry: 136n
Longhurst, 'Long John": 136n, 137n, 159n
Longmont, John: *see* Longhurst, ("Long John")
Loraine County, Ohio: 148n
Lorenzo (Jack County cowboy): 23–24
Los Angeles, Calif.: 140n
Lost Valley Fight: 50–53, 124n, 127n

Lost Valley Peak: 29
Louisville, Ky.: 119n
Loving, James C.: 4, 6, 18–22, 25, 28–29, 36, 49, 55, 117n, 123n, 124n, 127n, 129n
Loving, Oliver (father): 122n
Loving, Oliver (son): 127n, 130n
LX Ranch: 98, 156n, 157n

Mabry, Seth: 134n
McAllister, Daniel H.: 149n
McComas, C. C.: 151n
McGinnis (Jacksboro blacksmith): 122n
McIntire, Grace McColgin: 118n, 119n
McIntire, Isaac ("Jim"): book publication, 3, 117–18n; smallpox illness, 3, 103–112, 158n; errors of, 4, 122n, 124n–127n, 130n, 132n, 133n, 145n, 153n; described, 5–6, 154n; bigotry of, 6–7; death, 8; birth, 11, 118n; Ohio River adventures, 12–16, 119n, 120n; arrival in Texas, 16–17, 121n; work as cowboy, 18–19, 28, 31–35; Indian fights recounted, 20–27, 29–30, 50–56, 129n; hunting buffalo, 36–48, 125n; Texas Ranger service, 49–64, 126n, 127n, 133n, 134n, 140n, 144n; saloonkeeping, 65–68, 74–75; sheepherding, 68; as deputy sheriff, 68–71, 140n, 142n, 149n; arrests Wyatt Earp and Dave Mather, 70, 140n; as Las Vegas policeman, 72–74, 142n; as Lake Valley marshal, 75–78, 146n; as deputy U.S. marshal, 78, 149n; escape from New Mexico, 79–84, 149n, 150n; in riverboat wreck, 85; as gambler, 86, 90, 97, 99–102, 158n; arrested by Texas Rangers, 86, 151n, 152n; escape from Decatur jail, 87–90, 153n; arrested in New Orleans, 92–94, 154n; returned to New Mexico, 95–96, 155n, 156n; in shooting scrape, 97–99, 157n; philosophy of, 113–16; reports outlaw confederation, 136–37n, 159n; participation in Royal Gorge War, 137–38n
McIntire, James W.: 11, 118n, 119, 121n
McIntire, John: 118n
McIntire, Kittie: 8, 78–79, 84–85, 149n, 152, 158n
McIntire, Sarah: 119n
McIntire, William: 118n
McIntire Publishing Company: 117n, 118n
Maddox, Walter T. ("Jim"): 152n
Mamaday-te (Kiowa): 128n
Martin (Belknap merchant): 66–68
Mason, Barney: 143n
Mason, Mary (Mrs. Tom): 30, 125n

Mason, Tom: 29, 125n
Masterson, W. B. ("Bat"): 137n
Mather, "Mysterious Dave": 4, 70, 130n, 140n, 141n, 142n
Matthews, Joe: 132n
Maysville, Ky.: 120n
Medford, Okla.: 157n
Meeks family: 61, 131n
Memphis, Tenn.: 155n
Metcalf, Capt.: *see* Metcalf, Leonidas
Metcalfe, Leonidas: 15–16, 120n
Miami, Texas: 136n
Miami and Erie Canal: 15, 120n
Millett, Alonzo, Eugene, and Hiram: 65, 134n
Mimbres Apache Indians: 139n
Mississippi River: 91
Mississippi Valley Railroad: 155n
Mobeetie, Texas: 68–70, 78, 97, 117n, 118n, 134n, 135n, 137n–142n,
    146n, 157n, 158n
"Moderators": 62–63, 131n
Monongahela River: 85
Mont, J. J.: 136n, 137n, 159n
Montague, Texas: 61–62
Montague County, Texas: 29, 61, 62, 124n, 131n
Montauk County: 61–62
Montgomery, George A.: 135n
Moore, George: 128n
Moore, William C. ("Outlaw Bill"): 148n–151n, 156n
Mora, N.Mex.: 141n
Morgan, Gen. John H. (C.S.A.): 13, 119n, 133n
Morgan's Raid: 13, 119n, 133n
Morley, J. F.: 73, 144n
Morrison, A. L.: 148n
Mosely, George: 122n
Mountain View, Okla.: 102–103, 158n
Muldoon (Las Vegas posseman): 141n
Mulligan, George: 34
Murphy, Andrew H.: 154n
Murphy, John: 93, 154n

National Rifle Association: 126n
Navy revolver: 54

Needle gun: 54
Neill, Hyman G. ("Hoodoo Brown"): 143n
New Mexico Territorial Militia: 77–80, 83, 147n, 149n, 150n, 156n
Newby, Augustus J. ("Gus"): 151n
Newcomb, J. G. ("Ed"): 29, 124n
Newkirk, Okla.: 157n
New Orleans, La.: 16, 84, 91–94, 150n, 154n; *Daily Picayune*, 155n
No Man's Land: 69, 138n
Nolan, Capt. Nicolas (U.S.A.): 136n, 139n
Nolan County, Texas: 132n
Norton, A. B.: 138n, 139n, 146n
Nutt Station, N.Mex.: 78, 146n
Nye, W. S.: 128n, 130n

Ohio and Erie Canal: 15, 120n
Ohio No. 4 (riverboat): 15, 120n
Ohio River: 3, 6, 15, 85, 118n–120n, 159n
Oldham County, Texas: 156n

Palo Pinto (Paliponte), Texas: 4, 32, 34, 125n
Palo Pinto County, Texas: 50, 64, 122n, 125n, 127n, 133n, 147n
Panhandle and Santa Fe Railway: 157n
Panhandle City, Texas: 99, 101–102, 157n, 159n
Parish Prison, New Orleans, La.: 93–94, 155n
Patton, Lt.: 80, 149n
Pawnee, Okla.: 157n
Peak, Capt. Junius ("June") (Texas Ranger): 64, 126n, 133n
Pecora, Tony: 154n
Perkins, Lee N.: 61–62, 131n
Perry, Okla.: 157n
Phelon, Thomas: 156n
Pickett, Tom: 72, 142n, 143n
Pinkerton National Detective Agency: 4
Pittsburgh, Pa.: 85
Poe, John W.: 4, 70, 117n, 132n, 140n, 141n
Poindexter, George: 144n
Pomeroy, Ohio: 15, 119n, 120n
Porter, M. W. ("Mel"): 128n
Portsmouth, Ohio: 15, 120n
Potter County, Texas: 157n
Preston, James: 61, 131n

Pueblo, Colo.: 137n
Purdy, R. S.: 123n, 124n

Ragtown, Texas: 100, 157n
Randall, William ("Red"): 71, 141n
Reagan, Jim: 123n
"Reddish": 55–56, 130n
Red River: 16, 29, 124n, 156n
Reed, Mr.: 117n, 118n
"Regulators": 62–63, 131n
Remington rifle: 126n
Republican Party: 148n, 152n
Reynolds, A. E.: 125n
Reynolds, "Diamond Jo": 151n
Reynolds, Thomas: 154n
Rhinehart: *see* Rinehart, Ira
Richardson, T. C.: 117n, 146n
Richmond, Harry: 151n, 156n
Riley, Kinch: 138n
Riley, Tom: 69, 138n, 139n
Rinehart, Ira: 4, 69, 139n
Rio Grande: 145n
Roberts, Charley: 65–66
Roberts, Frank: 136n, 137n, 159n
Roberts, Gov. Oran M.: 131n
Roberts County, Texas: 136n
Robertson, Walter M.: 128n
Rocky Mountain Detective Agency: 149n
Rogers, C. T. (McIntire alias): 154n
Romero, Desiderio: 73–74, 143n
Roswell, N.Mex.: 70
Round Rock, Texas: 133n
Royal Gorge War: 138n
Rudabaugh, Dave: 4, 71–73, 130n, 141n–144n
Ruderbaugh, Dave: *see* Rudabaugh, Dave

Saint Louis, Mo.: 95, 138n
Salt Creek Prairie: 56
San Antonio, Texas: 68; *Daily Express*, 152n
San Miguel County, N.Mex.: 144n
Sanders, Cal: 123n

Santa Fe, N.Mex.: 73, 95, 144n, 149n, 155n
Satank (Kiowa): 127n
Satanta (Kiowa): 50, 54, 127n, 129n
Schmitt, Capt. George H. (Texas Ranger): 151n, 152n
Scioto River: 120n
Scott, Mueller W.: 149n, 156n
Selma, Ala.: 134n
Selman, John: 132n, 136n, 137n
Selman, "Tom Cat": 136n
Shackelford County, Texas: 63, 68, 124n, 132n, 133n, 136n
Shannon, John: 77, 147n, 150n
Sharp County, Ark.: 130n
Sharps rifle: 126n
Shedden, Jack: 78, 147–148n
Sheldon, Gov. Lionel Allen: 4, 78, 83, 94–96, 147n, 151n, 155n
Sheridan, Gen. Philip H. (U.S.A.): 129n
Shinplasters: 13, 16, 17, 48, 65, 120n, 159n
Short, Luke: 153n, 156n
Shreveport, La.: 16, 84, 91
Sierra Mining Company: 148n
Silliman, John: 132n, 136n, 137n
Simpson, Pete (sheriff): 149n
Siringo, Charles A.: 4–6, 8
Smallpox: 3, 4, 102, 103, 112, 137n, 158n
Smith, Billy: 136n
Smith, Buck: 132n, 136n, 137n
Smith, Corp. Jack (Texas Ranger): 133n
Smith, Lee: 141n
"Smoky Jim" (Panhandle gambler): 101–102, 157n
Socorro, N.Mex.: 74–75, 145n, 146n
Socorro Committee of Safety: 145n
Socorro County, N.Mex.: 149n
Socorro Stranglers: 145n
Socorro Sun: 145n
Spencer rifle: 21, 22, 54
Staked Plains: 4, 76, 98. 99, 147n, 156n
Stanley, F.: *see* Crocchiola, Fr. Stanley
Starbird, Nelson W.: 144n
Steele, Adj. Gen. William: 123n, 127n
Steele, William, Jr.: 72, 143n, 145n
Stephens, Capt. G. W. (Texas Ranger):128n

Stewart, Frank: 142 n, 143 n
Stinking Springs, N.Mex.: 143 n
Sweeney, Pat: 25–26
Sweetwater, Nolan County, Texas: 132 n, 134 n
Sweetwater, Wheeler County, Texas: *see* Mobeetie, Texas
Sweetwater Creek: 134 n

Tarrant County, Texas: 121 n, 153 n
Tascosa, Texas: 98, 136 n, 139 n, 156 n
Taylor, A. K.: 131 n
Terrell, Edward S.: 17, 39, 121 n
Texarkana, Texas: 130 n
Texas Cattle Raisers Association: 122 n
Texas Pacific Railroad: 91
Texas Rangers: 3, 49–65, 77, 83–84, 86–90, 118 n, 123 n, 124 n, 126 n–
    134 n, 136 n, 137 n, 140 n, 144 n, 145 n, 146 n, 151 n, 152 n, 153 n, 156 n
Thomasville, Ga.: 138 n
Thompson, Ben: 138 n
Thorp Spring: 64
T.I.C. Detective Agency: 153 n
Tickle, Henry: 89–90, 153 n
Tin Hat Band Brigade: 132 n
Tipton, Tobe: 123 n
Toledo, Ohio: 120 n
Tomb, A. D. ("Frosty"): 135 n
Tombstone, Ariz.: 140 n
Trinidad, Colo.: 141 n
Trinity River: 153 n
Trujillo (alleged killer of John Longhurst): 137 n

Union Pacific Railroad: 64, 133 n

Valdez, Antonio Lino: 143 n
Van Patton, Lt. Eugene (militia): 80, 149 n
Varden, Dolly: 135 n
Vernon, Texas: 98, 99, 156 n
Victorio (Apache): 139 n
Vigilantes: at Fort Griffin, 62–64, 131 n, 132 n, 133 n; at Socorro, 74–75,
    145 n

Wabash County, Ind.: 143 n

Ward, W. G.: 143n
Washburn, Texas: 100–101, 157n
Washington, D.C.: 78, 130n, 153n
Watts, John: 77, 147n, 150n
Wave, Matilda: 135n
Weatherford, Texas: 17–19, 121n, 122n
Webb, John Joshua: 73, 138n, 141n, 142n, 143n
Weed, W. H.: 117n, 118n
West, James: 71, 141n
Western Cattle Trail: 156n
Western Union Company: 11
West Point Academy: 138n
Wheeler County, Texas: 134n, 135n, 136n, 138n, 139n, 140n, 142n, 156n,
    157n
White (Lake Valley merchant): 78
White (rancher): see Wright, J. K. P
White, Mrs.: 21–22
White, Ellen: 119n
White, Johnny: 11–15, 119n
White, Knute: 26–27, 123n
White, Stephen: 119n
White Elephant saloons: Denison, Texas, 90, 153n; Fort Worth, Texas, 153n;
    Wichita Falls, Texas, 86, 151n, 153n
Whiteman (horse): 23
White Oaks, N.Mex.: 118n
Wichita County, Texas: 155n
Wichita Falls, Texas: 84, 86, 94, 151n, 153n
Wilbarger County, Texas: 156n, 157n
Wiley, Moses: 136n–137n
Wilkinson, Jim: 97
Willett (brother-in-law of J. C. Loving): 26–27, 123n
Willett, Mrs.: 21–22
Willett, Mary E. (Mrs. J. C. Loving): 123n
William Kiled: see *Will Kyle*
Williams, Benjamin: 135n
Will Kyle (riverboat): 84–85, 150n
Willot, Budd: 34, 125n
Wilson, Bill: 72, 142n, 143n
Wilson, Tom: 76–77, 147n
Wilson, Tom (sheriff): 50–51, 127n, 147n
Winchester rifle: 66, 97, 136n

Wise County, Texas: 129n
Woods, John H.: 148n, 149n
Woodward, Okla.: 8, 102, 157n, 158n
Woody, A. N.: 150n, 152n
Worcester, N.Y.: 148n
Wormwood, Henry: 123n
Wright, J. K. P.: 23–14, 123n

Yarberry (Yarborough), Milton J.: 4, 58–60, 130n, 156n
Young County, Texas: 121n, 124n, 126n